Mind Chess: Escaping the Game of the Covert Narcissist

MIND CHESS

First edition. December 22, 2024.

ISBN: 979-8230256175

Written by Nicole Elizabeth Orozco.

Table of Contents

Dedication

To those who light my world:

My beloved family - Chuck, Cheyne, Kristen, Ryan, Caitlin, Shelbi, Jake, Jasmine, Mila, Madden, Keegan, Kehlani, and Mo (Audrey). You are my heart walking in many bodies, my joy multiplied, my reason for growing stronger.

To my mother, Patricia Staniskis - your absence is a presence, your lessons echo in my choices, your love continues to guide me. I miss you more than words can say, and I couldn't have navigated this life without the foundation you built.

To those who have crossed the veil before us - family and friends whose fingerprints remain on my heart - you are not gone, just ahead on the path.

And to all who have walked this journey with me - you know who you are - thank you for being lights in both darkness and dawn.

Author's Note

There are some books that we write because we want to. This is one I wrote because I needed to. After decades of studying human behavior and psychology, I still fell into covert, narcissistic relationships, both personal and professional. This was despite years of work in various roles.

This isn't another book about narcissism. This is about the quiet ones, the "spiritual" ones, the ones who wound you with a whisper instead of a shout. They leave you questioning your sanity, all the while showing a façade of concern.

If you're reading this, chances are you've experienced it too. Maybe you're still in it. You want to know why something so perfect on the surface feels so wrong underneath. Maybe you've broken free and are trying to make sense of what happened. Or maybe you're starting to see patterns in your relationships that finally have a name.

I have scribed this from both personal experience and professional understanding. It's written with the rawness of someone who has been there and the insight of someone who has studied why. Most importantly, it aims to help end covert narcissistic abuse. This is not by becoming harder, but by becoming wiser.

This book comes from both wounds and wisdom. It is a product of hard lessons learned. Our struggles can help others. My hope is to help others by sharing these insights. I want them to: 1. Recognize patterns I missed. 2. Trust instincts I doubted. 3. Find strength they didn't know they had.

What you'll find in these pages isn't theory. It's real life. It's messy. It's complicated. And it's hopeful. Understanding covert narcissism isn't about spotting abuse. It's about reclaiming your power, your voice, and your right to be yourself.

Let's begin this journey together.

NICOLE ELIZABETH OROZCO

Introduction: Escaping the Game of Control

Let's talk about something possibly affecting your life right now, even if you don't realize it. Do you know that feeling in your gut when something's just off? When you're giving and giving, trying so hard to keep the peace, just trying to do the right thing, but somehow you end up feeling drained, confused, and maybe even a little crazy? Yeah, that feeling. We need to talk about that.

I've been there – oh boy, have I been there. As an empath (and if you're reading this book, chances are you might be one, too), I've been like a magnet for narcissists my entire life. The obvious ones, sure – those loud, look-at-me types who need to be the center of everything. But the sneaky ones? The quiet ones who seem so sweet, giving, and concerned about everyone else? They're the ones who really got me. And that's why I had to write this book.

Here's the thing: narcissism doesn't wear a name tag. It doesn't introduce itself at parties saying, "Hi, I'm here to slowly drain your soul while making you think it's all your fault!" No, it shows up as your super-helpful coworker who always makes you feel like you're not doing enough. It's that friend who's always there for you until you're completely exhausted from maintaining the friendship. It's that partner who seems so sensitive and caring but leaves you wondering why you're always walking on eggshells.

Let me tell you a story. I used to have this friend – let's call her Sarah. Everyone loved Sarah. She was always organizing fun get-togethers, remembering everyone's birthdays, and being there for every crisis. She seemed like the perfect friend. But after every interaction, I felt... depleted. Sometimes, I couldn't even explain why. She was so nice! How could I possibly complain about someone so giving? It took me years to understand that her "giving" came with invisible strings, and those strings were slowly turning into chains.

This book is crucial because right now, someone reading this is nodding their head, feeling that knot in their stomach, thinking, "Oh my God, this is my life." It could be your boss, your mom, your spouse. These are the people who seem caring and supportive but leave you feeling inadequate and drained. If this resonates with you, this book is for you.

It's important for you to know that you're not alone in this. You're not crazy, you're not too sensitive. There are others who have experienced what you're going through, and we're here to support you.

We all have some narcissistic traits – that's normal. Sometimes, we all get self-centered, need attention, or fail to see others' perspectives. But there's a world of difference between having some traits and being a covert narcissist who systematically breaks down others' sense of self. It's like the difference between occasionally overeating cake and having a severe eating disorder. One is normal human behavior; the other is a pattern that destroys lives.

As empaths, we're especially vulnerable. We're the peacekeepers, the ones who want everyone to be happy and who'll twist ourselves into pretzels trying to maintain harmony. We hate conflict so much that we'll ignore red flags the size of Texas to keep the peace. We're smart, capable people in so many areas of our lives, but when it comes to dealing with covert narcissists, our greatest strengths – empathy, compassion, and the desire to help – become the very things that can be used against us.

I've been that churchgoing "good person" who thought serving others meant letting myself be used up. I've been that employee working nights and weekends because my boss was "counting on me" and "knew I was the only one who could handle it." I've been that friend who kept giving and giving because "that's what good friends do."

Let me be clear: there's nothing wrong with being giving, kind, or hardworking. The problem comes when these beautiful qualities are exploited by people who know exactly how to use them for their benefit while keeping their mask of humble servitude.

Do you know what opened my eyes? When I started talking about this with other people. Once I began sharing my experiences, the stories just poured out. It was like opening a floodgate. Sharing our experiences is not just cathartic, it's a powerful tool for understanding and healing.

Take my friend Jessica's story. She had this business partner who initially seemed like a dream come true. "He was so humble," she told me. "Always giving credit to others, always talking about how blessed he was to work with such talented people." But slowly, things started shifting. Important meetings would get scheduled when she couldn't make them. Decisions would be made without her input, but if she brought it up, he'd say things like, "Oh, I thought we discussed that... you seemed so overwhelmed, I didn't want to burden you further." After two years, she found herself pushed out of major decisions in her own company while he kept his reputation as the most considerate, thoughtful business partner anyone could ask for.

Or listen to Mark's experience with his covert narcissist wife: "Everyone thought I had the perfect marriage. Kylee always posted on social media about how grateful she was for me and how blessed she felt. But behind closed doors? She'd spiral into a crisis if I didn't respond to her texts immediately. If I spent time with my friends, she'd get 'mysteriously' ill. She never directly yelled or demanded anything – she was too 'spiritual.' Instead, she'd talk about how sensitive she was, how deeply she felt things, and how her need for connection differed from other people's. I ended up isolated from everyone I loved, walking on eggshells in my own home and still feeling like I was the problem."

Then there's Maria's story about her mother: "My mom was the church volunteer queen. Everyone called her an angel. She spent her life 'serving others,' but at home? Every good deed came with a price tag of guilt. 'Oh, I'm so tired from helping Sister Johnson today, but don't worry about me...' or 'I gave up my dreams to raise you children, but that's what a good mother does...' It took me years of therapy to understand that true giving doesn't come with a side of manipulation."

These stories might sound familiar to you. It could be too familiar. You may be sitting there thinking about your situation, wondering if that person in your life who seems so perfect on the surface might be slowly draining your soul.

Let me tell you something important: Recognizing the pattern is the first step to freedom. That's why this book matters, and understanding the game of covert narcissistic control is crucial.

Think about it like this: Knowing the rules gives you an advantage when you're playing a game. But with covert narcissists they're playing a game where they know all the rules, and they've deliberately kept you in the dark. They're counting on your good nature, desire to see the best in people, and willingness to give second (and third, and fourth) chances.

I remember the moment it clicked for me. I was sitting in my car after another exhausting interaction with my "giving" friend, feeling that familiar mixture of guilt and depletion, when I suddenly thought, "Why do I feel so bad after spending time with someone who's supposedly so good to me?" That question changed everything.

This book is your guide to understanding the game you didn't even know you were playing. It's about recognizing the subtle tactics, understanding the patterns, and – most importantly – learning how to protect yourself without losing your beautiful ability for empathy and compassion.

Here's the truth: You can keep your caring heart while developing a stronger spine, remain compassionate while setting healthy boundaries, and honor your giving nature while protecting your energy.

How to Use This Guide

I KNOW PICKING UP THIS book might feel overwhelming. Maybe you're hiding it from someone. You may be reading it on your phone where nobody sees the title. Perhaps you're not even sure if you should be reading it at all – after all, isn't it mean to think someone might be a narcissist? (Spoiler alert: that guilt you're feeling? It's part of why covert narcissists have been able to fly under your radar for so long.)

This book isn't your typical self-help book; you don't need to read it from cover to cover. Think of it as a survival manual – you can jump to the most important chapters. Are you in a crisis with a covert narcissist boss? Head straight to the survival chapters. Are you realizing your best friend might be slowly driving you crazy? In the following chapters there is guidance on friendship and social manipulation. Dealing with family drama? We've got that covered, too.

Here's how I suggest using this book:

First, read through the stories. Highlight the ones that make your stomach clench with recognition. You know that feeling—when something resonates so deeply that it's like someone turned on a light in a dark room? Pay attention to those moments. They're your intuition finally getting the validation it's been craving.

Keep a journal as you read. I know, I know – another thing to do, right? But trust me on this. Covert narcissists are experts at making you doubt your reality. Writing things down helps you maintain your grip on the truth. Use it to record your "aha" moments, your memories that suddenly make sense, and the patterns you start recognizing in your life.

Don't beat yourself up as you read. You'll probably have moments of thinking, "How did I not see this sooner?" or "Why did I let this go on for so long?" We all have those thoughts. I certainly did. Remember: covert narcissists are experts at what they do, and your capacity for seeing the good in others is not a character flaw – it's been exploited by someone who knows how to use it against you.

Take breaks when you need to. Some of these revelations might hit hard, and that's okay. Sometimes, understanding the truth about someone in your life can feel like grieving. Permit yourself to process these emotions at your own pace.

Share what you're learning with trusted friends – emphasis on trusted. Be selective about who you talk to. Remember, covert narcissists often create wide social networks of people who only see their public mask. Choose confidants who have shown they can hold space for brutal truths.

Most importantly, start implementing what you learn immediately. You don't have to make huge, dramatic changes all at once. Small steps count. Each boundary you set, each time you trust your gut, each moment you choose to protect your energy—it all adds up.

A Note on Healing and Hope

HERE'S SOMETHING THAT kept me up at night when I first started understanding covert narcissism: "If I accept that this person is hurting me, does that mean everything was fake? Was any of it real?"

Let me share something important: Healing doesn't mean erasing all the good memories. It doesn't mean you have to rewrite your entire history. That friend who helped you through your divorce might still have been genuinely supportive AND be a covert narcissist who later used that vulnerability against you. That parent who paid for your college might have genuinely wanted the best for you AND used that generosity as a control tool. Both things can be true.

The path to healing isn't about becoming cynical or hard-hearted. God knows that was my first instinct! After realizing how many covert narcissists I'd attracted into my life, I wanted to build walls so high nobody could ever get close enough to hurt me again. But that's not healing – that's hiding.

Authentic healing is about getting better at reading the signs while keeping your heart open. It's about developing what I call your "emotional smoke detector." You know how a smoke detector doesn't prevent you from cooking – it just warns you when something's burning? That's what we're aiming for here. You can still love, give, and care deeply about others. You'll improve at noticing when something's not right before the whole house is on fire.

And let me tell you something that gives me hope: Once you understand this pattern, you can't unsee it. It's like getting glasses for the first time and realizing trees have individual leaves! Sure, it might be overwhelming initially, but that clarity is a gift. Each time you spot a covert narcissist's tactic, each time you maintain a boundary, each time you trust your gut – you're healing.

I had a client named Lisa who felt crazy for years because of her supposedly "perfect" marriage. She told me something beautiful recently. She said, "I can feel peace and chaos simultaneously for the first time in my life. I can recognize what happened to me AND still believe in love. I'm not angry anymore – I'm aware. And awareness is my superpower now."

That's what I want for you: not just survival but transformation, not just escape but enlightenment, not just healing but thriving.

As we go through this book together, you'll have moments of anger, sadness, and maybe even grief. That's normal. You might also have moments of incredible relief—finally understanding why you've felt so crazy all these years. Welcome all of it. Each emotion is part of your healing journey.

Here's what I know for sure: You're stronger than you think. The fact that you're reading this book proves you're ready to see the truth. And once you see it, once you understand the game of covert narcissistic control; That's when everything starts to change.

Are you ready? Let's dive in...

Chapter 1: Understanding the Player Behind the Mask

You know that moment when you're watching a magician, and even though you're looking right at their hands, you still can't see how they did the trick? That's what it's like dealing with a covert narcissist. Unlike their flashier cousins – the overt narcissists who need to be the loudest, brightest star in the room – covert narcissists are the ultimate sleight-of-hand artists. They're masters of the subtle, the quiet, the "who, me?" school of manipulation.

Let me tell you about my old boss, David. Everyone loved David. He was the leader who remembered your kids' names, brought coffee for the team during late nights, and always deflected praise to others. "Oh, I'm just blessed to work with such talented people," he'd say. Sounds wonderful, right?

But here's what was really happening: Those late nights? They became increasingly frequent because David would "humbly" mention how he was staying late too (guilt trip). That deflected praise? It came with subtle reminders of how much he'd done to "develop" our talents (ownership). Those personal touches like remembering kids' names? They became ammunition for guilt when you needed to leave early for a school event ("I care so much about little Ella; I hate that this urgent project might keep you from her concert").

The Hidden Face of Narcissism

THIS IS WHAT MAKES covert narcissism so tricky to spot. It doesn't show up wearing a "look at me" t-shirt. Instead, it often wears a humble sweater and carries a serving tray. It's the mother who martyrs herself for her children while simultaneously undermining their independence. It's the friend who's always there to help during your crises but needs even more support during their constant emergencies.

Think about the differences:

Overt Narcissist: "I'm the best at everything!" Covert Narcissist: "I just try to help where I can... though nobody seems to appreciate how much I give..."

Overt Narcissist: "You're nothing without me!" Covert Narcissist: "I worry that you might struggle without my guidance..."

Overt Narcissist: "I deserve special treatment!" Covert Narcissist: "I don't need anything special... though others get recognized while I give silently..."

See the difference? Same destination, different paths.

The Difference Between Healthy Self-Interest and Narcissism

NOW, LET'S TALK ABOUT something important: we all have narcissistic traits. Yes, all of us. Having a healthy self-interest isn't only normal – it's necessary. Being able to say, "I'm good at this," or "I need help," or "I want recognition for my work" – that's healthy adult behavior.

Sophie, one of my counseling clients, struggled with this distinction. "But I like getting compliments," she told me. "Sometimes I even fish for them. Does that make me a narcissist?"

Here's the crucial difference: Healthy self-interest is about addition; narcissism is about subtraction. When you have healthy self-interest, your success doesn't require others' failure, your happiness doesn't demand others' misery, and your self-worth isn't built on others' insecurities.

Let me illustrate this with a real-life example. In my early career, I had two mentors: Karen and Linda. Both were successful, took pride in developing new talent, and wanted recognition for their work.

Karen (healthy self-interest) would say: "I'm proud of helping you develop that presentation skill. Let's make sure you're ready to shine in the meeting."

Linda (covert narcissist) would say: "I'm just happy to help... though it hurts that you didn't mention my guidance when the boss praised your presentation..."

See the difference? Karen's pride contributed to my success, while Linda's "humility" subtracted from it.

The Making of a Covert Narcissist

UNDERSTANDING HOW COVERT narcissists are created helps us spot them better. Usually, their story involves either excessive praise or excessive criticism in childhood – sometimes both. They learn early that their true self isn't acceptable, so they develop this humble, giving persona as a survival mechanism.

I remember Tom, a covert narcissist I briefly dated years ago, sharing his background: "My mother always said I was special, different from other kids. But nothing I did was ever quite good enough. So, I learned to be the helper, the good boy, the one who never needed anything." Classic, right?

This brings us to something crucial: covert narcissists often honestly believe their own press. They're not usually conscious manipulators. They genuinely see themselves as humble servants who deserve (but never get) recognition for their sacrifices.

The Martyr Complex and False Humility

OH, THE MARTYR COMPLEX – this is where covert narcissists really shine. They're not just willing to help but eager to suffer for it. Then, they get to wear their suffering like an invisible crown.

My former friend Rachel was an expert at this. She'd volunteer for every challenging task, take on everyone's problems, and then spend weeks subtly reminding everyone of her sacrifices. "No, no, don't worry about me being exhausted. Helping others is its own reward..." *cough, martyr, cough.*

This false humility is like a superpower. It's so effective because it seems so virtuous on the surface. Who can criticize someone for being too giving, humble, or self-sacrificing?

The Wounded Healer Syndrome

THIS IS A FASCINATING subset of covert narcissism, and it's especially common in helping professions. These are the therapists, life coaches, spiritual leaders, or mentors who use their "healing journey" to maintain control and superiority.

I encountered this with a spiritual advisor who constantly referenced her own trauma to position herself as both wounded and wise. "I understand your pain so deeply... my own journey has been so challenging... that's why I can guide you..." Everything came back to her story, her wisdom, and her unique understanding.

Key Traits and Behaviors to Watch For

Let's break down some specific behaviors that might help you spot a covert narcissist:

1. They're energy barometers - always attuned to and affected by others' moods
2. They give advice without being asked
3. They help in ways that create dependency
4. They have an uncanny ability to make everything about them - even your successes and struggles
5. They're masters of subtle criticism disguised as concern
6. They collect grievances while presenting as forgiving
7. They're often found in helping roles or positions of subtle influence
8. They have a pattern of long-term relationships where they're the "giver" who's never appreciated enough

The Secret Superiority Complex

Here's the real kicker about covert narcissists: underneath all that humble pie is a steel-clad belief in their own superiority. They don't need to announce it like their overt cousins because they're sure.

A covert narcissist might say: "I just want everyone to get along," while thinking, "These people could never handle conflict as wisely as I do."

They might say, "I'm just here to support others," while believing, "No one else is as spiritually/emotionally/intellectually evolved as I am."

My friend Abby had a spiritual advisor who did this. She finally caught on when she realized that every story, piece of advice, and "humble" sharing circled back to the advisor's superior insight and understanding.

Marriage and Romantic Relationships

TAKE MY FRIEND MIKE'S marriage. His wife seemed like the most understanding, patient partner anyone could ask for. "I'm just trying to help you be your best self," she'd say. Sounds supportive, right? But here's how it actually played out:

If Mike got a promotion: "I'm so proud of how my support has helped you grow." If Mike made a friend: "I worry about their influence on you... I just understand you so much deeper than they can." If Mike wanted to try something new: "Oh honey, I don't want you to get hurt... remember what happened last time when you didn't take my advice?"

Every success became her success. Every independent choice became a risk. Every relationship became a threat. All wrapped up in this beautiful package of "caring" and "support."

The Workplace Wonder

THEN THERE'S THE COVERT narcissist at work – let me tell you about Patricia, a team leader I once had. She was the queen of what I call "helpful sabotage." She'd say things like:

"I'll help you with that presentation... I know how nervous you get." "Let me handle that client... you've been so stressed lately." "I added myself to your project... just to make sure you're supported."

She proclaimed herself as an outstanding mentor, dedicated to fostering the growth of others. Yet, her team members seemed to struggle to reach a level of independence that would validate her claims. This contradiction begs the question-how effective was she really in developing others?

There have been times when I've exhibited these behaviors, and I've had to confront my own narcissistic tendencies. The distinction between myself and the pathological covert narcissist is the distinct difference in that I actively engage in self-reflection and strive to overcome my character defects. You're not alone if you're reading this and identifying with these traits. Many of us are on a similar journey of self-improvement.

The "Spiritual" Friend

OH BOY, THIS ONE'S a doozy. My friend Kate had a "spiritual mentor" named Rebecca, who was the perfect example of covert narcissism wrapped in cosmic wisdom. Rebecca never claimed to be unique – no, no, she was just a "humble vessel for divine wisdom." But somehow:

- Every piece of advice came with a story about Rebecca's superior spiritual insight
- Every challenge was an opportunity for Rebecca to demonstrate her deeper understanding
- Every success in Kate's life was because she "finally followed Rebecca's guidance."
- Every struggle was because Kate "still had so much to learn."

The Parent Trap

THIS ONE HITS HOME for so many people. The covert narcissist parent doesn't say, "I'm better than you." Instead, they say things like:

"I just want what's best for you" (translation: I know better than you). "I've sacrificed everything for you" (translation: You owe me eternal devotion). "Nobody will ever love you like I do" (translation: Nobody should ever be more important than me)

I remember Rene's mom, who turned every holiday into an Olympic event of martyrdom: "Oh no, don't help with dinner. I'll do it all myself... like always." "Don't worry about visiting more often. I'll sit here alone... I'm used to it." "Of course, your in-laws can have Christmas morning. I'll have my little celebration alone..."

The Helper Friend

THIS ONE'S PARTICULARLY sneaky because it masquerades as the perfect friendship. They're always there when you need them – actually, they're there even when you don't need them. They show up uninvited during your crises because "that's what real friends do."

I had a friend like this – let's call her Maggie. She was the first to show up during any crisis and organized meal trains and support groups. Sounds impressive, right? But here's the catch: every act of help came with an invisible price tag of obligation. Every crisis became a story about her heroic friendship. Whenever you tried to help her back, it was never good enough compared to her "selfless giving."

The Professional Martyr Maker

LET ME SHARE SOMETHING personal here. I fell into the martyr role in my business partnership, but here's the twist – I wasn't born a martyr. I was created one, and maybe you can relate to how it happened.

It started with me just being enthusiastic about our work. I had the skills, the drive, and a tendency to take on too much (hey, we're all a work in progress, right?). But my partner? She was an artist at making her lack of contribution seem inevitable and somehow my choice.

Picture this: I'm working late on our projects, drowning in deadlines, while she's:

- Taking luxurious baths and getting her nails done
- Always having some personal drama that needed attention
- Constantly flattering me about how "amazing" I was at everything
- Playing up how she was "just not good with computers."
- Making promises to help that somehow never materialized
- Showing up like a star at public events, taking credit for work she never touched

The crazy part? She managed to make me feel both indispensable and invisible at the same time. When I'd ask for help, there was always a reason why she couldn't: "That's not a priority right now," or "You're so much better at this than me," or "I'm dealing with [insert latest drama]."

And here's where it gets really twisted: The more she didn't do, the more I did. The more I did, the more resentful I became. The more resentful I became, the more I looked like the bad guy. See how that works? While she maintained her serene, positive image, I turned into precisely what she needed me to be: the overworked martyr who could then be labeled as negative or difficult. And what is even crazier is that I became what I detested, and everyone around me could feel my energy. This was not good at all.

It's like the perfect crime. The covert narcissists hand you the rope one compliment at a time, watch you tie yourself up to prove your worth, then stand back, concerned about your "perfectionist tendencies" or "inability to delegate."

Looking back now, I can see how masterfully she played it. Whenever I tried to set a boundary, she'd dangle that carrot of future participation: "I'll definitely help with the social media next week!" Spoiler alert: Next week never came.

The lesson here? Sometimes, being a martyr isn't a personality trait you're born with – it's a role you're skillfully maneuvered into by someone who benefits from your sacrifice while maintaining their image as the peaceful, balanced one.

So now we understand that covert narcissism isn't just about someone being quietly self-centered. It's a sophisticated dance of false humility, carefully crafted helplessness and strategic martyrdom. But this is just scratching the surface.

In the next sections, we're going to dive deeper into what makes covert narcissists so different from their more obvious cousins. We'll look at that mask of humility they wear perfectly - the one that makes everyone else say, "But they're so nice!" when you try to explain what's happening. We'll explore why these subtle manipulators are so much harder to spot than the loud, obvious narcissists who need to be the star of every show.

Most importantly, we'll unpack how they maintain that wounded facade while controlling everything and everyone around them. Once you understand this—really understand it—you'll never be able to unsee it. And that's exactly what we need.

Remember, recognizing these patterns isn't about becoming paranoid or suspicious of everyone who acts humble. It's about developing a clearer picture of the difference between genuine humility and the kind used as camouflage. Think of it as getting a new pair of glasses - the world doesn't change, but your ability to see it clearly does.

Ready to dive deeper? Let's pull back that mask of humility and examine what's really going on underneath.

The Mask of Humility

"OH NO, I COULDN'T POSSIBLY take credit for that project..." "I'm just blessed to be able to help others..." "You're all so kind to notice my small contribution..."

Sound familiar? If these phrases make you think of someone in your life while giving you an uneasy feeling in your gut, buckle up. We're about to talk about one of the most effective disguises in the narcissist's wardrobe: the mask of humility.

Let me tell you about Josh, my former colleague. Josh was everyone's favorite team member. He was always the first to deflect praise, the last to take credit, and seemingly the most selfless person in any room. His favorite phrase? "I'm just happy to serve the team."

But here's what was happening: Every time Josh deflected praise, he drew more attention to his contribution. His humility wasn't a cloth covering but a spotlight with a dimmer switch. He'd say things like, "Oh, Madison did all the work..." (pause for everyone to disagree) "...I just stayed late every night for three weeks to support her vision." See what happened there?

This mask of humility is brilliant because it serves multiple purposes:

- It makes them appear more praiseworthy (because who doesn't love a humble person?)
- It creates an obligation for others to praise them more ("No,

Josh, you did so much!")
- It gives them a moral high ground to judge others from
- It makes anyone who questions them look petty or jealous

The really tricky part? Sometimes, they believe in their own press. They've worn the mask so long that it's become their face. They genuinely see themselves as humble servants while simultaneously expecting constant recognition for their humility.

Let me tell you about Claire. Everyone wanted to be in Claire's orbit. She had this way about her – this special glow that made you feel chosen to be near her. "I'm just drawn to special souls," she'd say, making everyone around her feel like they were part of some exclusive spiritual club.

Claire had a "calling," you see. A divine purpose. She was here to change lives, uplift others, and create something magical. And if you were lucky enough to be part of her inner circle, you got to be part of that magic, too.

Here's how she worked her magic:

"You have such a unique gift," she'd tell you, her eyes sparkling with what seemed like genuine admiration. "I can see it so clearly. That's why I feel called to work with you." And just like that, you'd feel seen. Special. Chosen.

But here's where it gets interesting. Despite the talk about your gifts, you do all the work. "You're just so much better at the details than I am," she'd sigh. "I'm more of a big-picture person, you know? I need to stay in my creative energy."

And when the work wasn't perfect? Oh, she had a way of delivering criticism that felt like a warm hug while leaving bruises: "I know you tried your best, sweetie. Maybe next time we should..." (Translation: not good enough) "I feel like this could be elevated a bit more..." (Translation: do it again) "I trust you'll figure it out..." (Translation: don't bother me with questions)

The real art was in how she kept everyone hooked. When you were ready to give up, she'd swoop in with that magnetic energy: "I don't know what I'd do without you..." "You're the only one who really understands my vision..." "We're creating something so special together..."

And the flattery? It was like emotional cocaine. She'd build you up in front of others, making you feel part of something bigger than yourself. But somehow, despite all your work, she remained the sun that everyone orbited around.

The meetings at her house were a perfect example. While everyone else was frantically working on "the mission," she'd be on her phone looking at shoes, occasionally dropping wisdom bombs like, "I'm getting a divine download about this..." or "The universe is guiding us to..."

And here's the genuinely masterful part: if you ever questioned anything, she'd look at you with such genuine confusion and hurt that you'd end up apologizing. "I'm just trying to create something beautiful for all of us," she'd say softly, making you feel small for even doubting.

Her closest circle became her unpaid staff, really. There was always someone managing her schedule, someone handling her emails, someone organizing her events – all while she kept this ethereal presence above it all. "I'm just so blessed to attract such capable people," she'd say, floating through rooms in flowing clothes, dispensing wisdom and gentle criticism like a spiritual CEO.

The wild part? Even when you were exhausted, frustrated, and questioning everything, she knew exactly how to pull you back in: "I had a dream about your role in all this..." "The universe specifically showed me your part in this journey..." "No one else quite understands the vision like you do..."

And those group meetings? Pure theater. She'd sit there, seemingly passive, while orchestrating everything. Someone would suggest an idea, and she'd tilt her head thoughtfully: "Interesting... what does everyone else feel about that?" Translation: this isn't what I want, but I will let the group shoot it down so I don't have to be the bad guy.

The really crazy-making part was watching her with newcomers. You'd see the whole cycle beginning again—the special attention, the spiritual connection, the gentle guidance into exhaustion—and if you tried to warn them, well, you'd just sound jealous or "low vibe."

Look, here's the thing: This kind of covert narcissist isn't just wearing a mask of humility – they're wearing a whole spiritual costume, complete with special effects and a supporting cast they've carefully trained to maintain their illusion.

This brings us to something crucial: How is this different from the obvious, out-there narcissists bragging about their achievements and openly demanding attention? Trust me, while they might look completely different on the surface, they're two sides of the same coin. Let's talk about how these covert operators differ from their more obvious cousins.

How Covert Narcissism Differs from Overt Narcissism

PICTURE TWO CONDUCTORS leading an orchestra. The first one (the overt narcissist) is all dramatic flourishes and bold movements, demanding everyone watch their brilliance. The second one (our covert friend) appears to barely move at all, yet somehow controls every note through subtle gestures and meaningful glances. Same music, a completely different show.

Let me break this down with something that happened in my wellness community. We had two prominent teachers: Brad and Savannah.

Brad (our overt narcissist) was all about his credentials, his followers, and his amazing achievements. "I've trained with the best!

My methods are revolutionary! Look at my before-and-after photos!" Classic stuff, right?

Then there was Savannah (our covert player). "I'm just sharing what spirit moves me to share," she'd say softly. "I don't believe in titles or hierarchy." Yet somehow, by the end of every session, everyone knew that:

- She'd had profound spiritual experiences others could only dream of
- Her methods were channeled from higher sources
- Only the truly evolved could grasp her subtle work

The same need for admiration in a totally different delivery system.

Here's what it looks like in practice:

Overt Narcissist: "I'm the best at what I do!" Covert Narcissist: "I just feel called to serve... though it's lonely sometimes being the only one who sees things at this level..."

Overt Narcissist: "You need me!" Covert Narcissist: "I worry about how you'll manage this journey without proper guidance..."

Overt Narcissist: "Nobody else comes close to my expertise!" Covert Narcissist: "It's not about expertise... I have a different level of awareness that comes from my deep inner work..."

The overt narcissist will tell you they're special. The covert narcissist will make you tell them they're special. And if you don't? That shows you're not evolved enough to recognize their true gifts.

It's like they both want to be seen as the star of the show, but while the overt narcissist grabs the spotlight, the covert narcissist claims they're actually glowing from within. Same destination, different paths.

Ah yes, let me paint these perfect examples of the differences:

While the overt narcissist is bragging about running the event, our covert friend plays it differently:

Picture this: The whole team has been working on a significant event for weeks. Martha (our covert narcissist) looks fresh and fabulous while everyone else is exhausted. She works the room masterfully: "Oh, you're all so amazing! I don't know how you do it!" (While everyone's thinking: Where were you during setup?)

Here's the real art of it: "I just couldn't get my part done because I've been so overwhelmed..." (Cue sympathetic looks) "Technology just isn't my thing... could you show me one more time?" (For the fifteenth time) "I meant to do those social media posts, but with everything going on..." (Vague reference to unnamed dramas)

The procrastination dance is particularly clever:

- Monday: "I'm just not feeling aligned with the energy today..."
- Wednesday: "I had to do my bed sheets today, we should wait..."
- Friday: "Oh, you did it already? You're such a lifesaver!"

And here's where it differs from the overt Narcissist's approach:

Overt narcissist in a Crisis: "None of you know what you're doing! I have to do everything myself!"

Covert narcissist in a crisis: "I'm just so overwhelmed... everything keeps going wrong... I don't know how I attract such tricky situations..." (Meanwhile, you're scrambling to fix their manufactured or real crisis – for the hundredth time, while they're getting sympathy from everyone else)

The competence contradiction is fascinating: "I'm just not good with spreadsheets..." (Until they need to prove you did something wrong) "You know I struggle with technology..." (But somehow manages perfect social media posts of their dog) "I need you to handle all the details..." (But will criticize every single one)

The entitlement shows up differently, too. While the overt narcissist demands special treatment, our covert friend: "I know it's last minute, but with everything I'm going through..." (Cue sad eyes) "I would never ask, but since you're so good at this..." (Flattery + burden =

their favorite combo) "I know this sounds weird but God is telling me to step back and let others handle this..." (How convenient)

And here's the expert stroke: At the end of every project, event, and crisis, they somehow emerge as both the victim and the hero of the story. While the overt narcissist shouts, "I did it all!" our covert friend sighs, "We did it... despite all the challenges I had to overcome..." (conveniently forgetting that most of those challenges were their own creation).

This is what makes covert narcissists so much harder to spot than their overt cousins. They play chess while the overt narcissist is playing checkers. Every move is subtle, every manipulation wrapped in a soft blanket of victimhood and charm.

But to understand how deep this goes, we must look at what's behind both the wounded facade and the controlling core. That's where the real game is played—in the space between their carefully crafted image of vulnerability and their iron-clad need for control.

The Wounded Facade versus the Controlling Core

LET ME TELL YOU ABOUT "The Wounded Bird Act." When someone seems fragile and hurt by life, you want to help them—only to eventually realize you're the one with clipped wings.

Here's how it typically plays out. The covert narcissists present themselves as survivors of something – difficult childhoods, toxic relationships, misunderstood geniuses, or spiritual warriors who've "been through so much." Their pain becomes their passport to special treatment.

"I just feel things so deeply," they'll say, eyes glistening with well-timed tears. "Not everyone understands how sensitive I am..."

But watch what happens when you look closer. That same person who's "too wounded" to handle essential responsibilities somehow has the energy to:

- Micromanage everyone else's efforts
- Criticize work they didn't do
- Create elaborate dramas requiring everyone's attention
- Control every situation from behind their tissue box

I had a business partner like this—let's call her Grace. She was always "too overwhelmed" to handle client emails but somehow had the bandwidth to critique every response I wrote. "I just care so deeply about getting it right," she'd say, adding hours to my workload with her "suggestions."

The real mastery is how they use their wounds to keep control: "I would help, but after what I've been through..." "My anxiety makes it impossible for me to..." "My healing journey requires me to..."

Meanwhile, your healing journey? Your needs? Your boundaries? Those are just inconvenient obstacles to their control.

This makes this so crazy-making: their wounds are always bigger than yours. Had a bad day? They're having an existential crisis. Feeling sick? They have three mysterious ailments that doctors can't diagnose. Setting a boundary? You're triggering their deep-seated abandonment issues.

Let me give you a perfect example. My former mentor, Diana, was "too traumatized" by past betrayals to handle confrontation. Yet somehow, she managed to:

- Send detailed criticism via 2AM emails
- Create elaborate rules about how others should behave around her
- Orchestrate complex social situations where others did her dirty work

- Maintain iron-clad control over her image while appearing "too fragile" to handle conflict

The control shows up in fascinating ways: "I wish I could join the meeting, but my energy is so sensitive..." (Translation: You'll have to come to brief me personally later) "My trauma makes it hard to handle details..." (Translation: You do it, but I'll criticize how you do it) "I'm too overwhelmed to deal with this right now..." (Translation: Drop everything and manage my crisis)

And here's the really clever part—they use their wounds to keep control even over how you respond to their power: "You know how fragile I am right now..." "I thought you understood my struggles..." "I'm just trying to protect my peace..."

It's like emotional hostage-taking, wrapped in a comfort blanket of victimhood.

And if you dare to point out that they seem perfectly capable of control when they want it? Watch how quickly the wounded facade and controlling core switch places: "I can't believe you'd attack someone who's been through what I have..." "This is exactly why I have trust issues..." "I guess I need to protect myself more..." (Translation: Prepare for punishment)

The wounded facade isn't just a mask – it's a weapon, a shield, and a control mechanism. While the overt narcissist uses evident power to control, the covert narcissist uses apparent powerlessness to achieve the same goal.

And here's what makes this wounded facade/control dynamic so effective: it creates the perfect trap. If you try to help the person, you're enabling their control. If you try to set boundaries, you're "attacking" someone who's already wounded. If you point out their manipulation, you're "just like all the others who've hurt them."

It's like they've created a game in which they're both the ultimate victim and the ultimate authority on everyone else's reality. Their wounds become their credentials, armor, and weapon—all while maintaining the appearance of someone who just needs a little more understanding, a little more help, and a little more accommodation.

This brings us to perhaps the most critical question: Why are these masters of disguise so much harder to spot than their overt counterparts? Understanding this isn't just about recognizing their tactics—it's about understanding why so many smart, caring, capable people find themselves caught in their web before they even realize there is a spider.

Let's talk about why these emotional sleight-of-hand artists are so much harder to identify than classic narcissists and why even therapists and counselors sometimes miss the signs...

Why Coverts are Harder to Identify than Classic Narcissists

LET ME PAINT YOU A scene that might feel painfully familiar. You've asked your "collaborative" partner for something completely reasonable – maybe a simple spreadsheet of expenses, basic login information, or to follow through on a task they promised to do.

Their response? Pure artistry in evasion: "Oh, I'm not really a details person..." "Can't you just handle that part? You're so good at it..." "I don't feel aligned with that energy right now..." "Why are you so focused on the small stuff?"

And somehow, you feel like you're the unreasonable one for asking.

Or how about those "playful" put-downs? You know the ones: "Oh, there goes [your name] being all Type A again! Isn't she adorable?" "We can't all be perfect like [your name] *wink wink*." "Someone's taking things a bit seriously today!"

It seems like friendly teasing, right? But it's death by a thousand cuts, each carefully designed to put you in your place while making you look oversensitive if you object.

The crisis requests are particularly masterful: "I know it's midnight, but I'm having a spiritual emergency..." "My computer crashed right before this deadline..." "Everything's falling apart, and you're the only one who can help..."

And the selective apologies? Pure genius: "I'm sorry if I seemed distant..." (But not sorry for missing another deadline) "I apologize for not being more present..." (But not for the manipulative behavior) "I could have communicated better..." (But not about the actual issue) which never gets addressed.

They've mastered all the correct language: "I'm all about authentic connections..." "I value radical honesty..." "I'm committed to conscious communication..."

Try to actually have an authentic, honest, conscious conversation about problems. Watch how fast they disappear: "I can't handle this energy right now..." "I'm choosing to protect my peace..." "We should wait until you're less emotional..."

And by the time you finally snap – after months or years of this dance – you look like the unstable one. They've created such a perfect paper trail of being the reasonable, spiritual, conscious one that your valid frustration seems to come out of nowhere.

The way they make us complicit is particularly devious. They create situations where you become a witness or unwitting participant in their games:

The web of complicity is woven so subtly, thread by thread. It starts with shared secrets: "Don't tell anyone, but..." They make you feel unique with selective trust: "I'm only sharing this with you because..." Before you know it, you're bound by these confidences, keeping their secrets, becoming part of their carefully constructed reality.

The manipulation deepens as they create situations where you become their unwitting accomplice. You find yourself covering for their missing work, explaining their absences, and defending their behavior to others. Each time you speak on their behalf, you become more deeply entangled in their web of deception.

Then comes the masterful setup: They push your buttons in private for months, creating pressure that builds until you finally react in public. When you do, they respond calmly: "I'm worried about you... you've seemed so stressed lately..." Their performance is perfect - they appear supportive, while you appear unstable.

When you realize what's happening, they've already crafted an airtight narrative. They have a documented history of being "supportive," while you appear increasingly "intense." Your attempts to explain the truth sound paranoid because who would believe this gentle, spiritual person could be so calculating?

The real artistry lies in how they convince you to doubt your perceptions. "You're just triggered right now." "This is your stuff coming up." You should examine why you're so angry. And when you finally gather the courage to confront them? They have an arsenal of responses: They need space to process. You're all mirrors for each other. They feel attacked. Or: That never happened.

This is why covert narcissists are so much harder to spot than their overt counterparts. While an overt narcissist plays their game openly, a covert narcissist creates an entirely different reality - one where they make all the rules while pretending they're not even playing. They gaslight you with a smile, undermine you with concern, and destroy your credibility while appearing to support you.

Remember: The reason you didn't spot it sooner isn't because you're naive or weak. It's because they're experts at what they do. They've spent years perfecting their technique, learning to appear vulnerable while maintaining control, seeming spiritual while manipulating others, and looking innocent while creating chaos.

The good news? Once you understand their playbook, you can't unsee it. That's why we spent this chapter breaking down their tactics in detail. In the coming chapters, we'll dive into specific strategies for protecting yourself, keeping your sanity, and breaking free from their web of control.

But for now, know this: That knot in your stomach? That feeling that something's off despite all evidence to the contrary? That's your intuition fighting through their manipulation. It's time to start trusting it.

In the next chapter, you will be shown exactly how they build their arsenal of control, but first, take a moment to acknowledge how far you've come just by recognizing these patterns. Understanding the game is the first step to stopping it.

Chapter 2: The Hidden Arsenal - Strategies of the Covert Player

You know when you leave a conversation feeling awful, but you can't quite understand why? Or when you apologize but aren't sure what you did wrong? Welcome to the covert narcissist's toolbox.

Think of this chapter as your field guide to their favorite weapons. These are not the overt tools of the narcissist—no shouting, no direct insults, no clear demands. They are more like emotional paper cuts, individually insignificant but devastating in their cumulative effect.

Let's break down their three most powerful tools:

- Subtle manipulation tactics (the art of making you think everything's your idea)
- Quiet guilt-tripping (death by a thousand "Oh, don't worry about me..." sighs)
- Hidden gaslighting techniques (making you doubt your reality without ever raising their voice)

Before we dive deep into each one, let me share a quick story that shows all three in action. A few years back, my colleague Jane worked on a project with a "collaborative" partner. Here's how one interaction went:

Partner (subtle manipulation): "You're much better at presentations than I am..." Jane: "We could work on it together?"

Partner (quiet guilt trip): "Oh, I wouldn't want to hold you back..." Jane: "You wouldn't be holding me back at all!" Partner (hidden gaslighting): "Didn't we discuss this last week? I thought you said you preferred doing these alone..."

By the end of that five-minute conversation, Jane was doing all the work, feeling guilty about not wanting to and questioning whether she had actually said she preferred working alone. Over time, this dynamic took a toll on Jane's mental health and self-esteem, as she began to doubt her own abilities and felt responsible for her partners feelings.

Let's unpack each of these tools in detail...

Subtle Manipulation Tactics: Creating Controlled Chaos

HERE'S SOMETHING THAT took me years to understand: when a covert narcissist seems nervous around certain people, pay attention. It's not because they're intimidated– they've spotted someone who might see through their game.

Let me share a situation that might feel familiar. We had three people in our business venture: me, Vicky (our covert narcissist), and Beth (the truth-teller). Beth had this annoying habit of... well, being direct. She'd say, "These numbers don't add up." "We need actual deadlines, not vague promises." "Why isn't this work getting done?"

Watch how Vicky played it: First, the private conversations: "I'm worried about Beth's energy..." "She seems so angry all the time..." "I feel like she's trying to create division..."

Then, the subtle alliance-building: "You and I just get each other..." "We have such a special connection..." "We deserve better than this negativity..."

The masterful part? Vicky would create situations where Beth would naturally get frustrated, then use Beth's reactions as proof of her "concerns":

- Ignoring Beth's ideas in meetings
- Making decisions without her input
- Creating delays that affected Beth's work
- Responding to Beth's direct questions with vague, unrelated answers

And here's where it gets tricky – I started acting like Vicky to deal with Beth. Why? Because Vicky had created this reality where Beth was the "problem," and I was trying to help manage the "problem." I found myself:

- Making excuses for Vicky's behavior
- Mediating conflicts Vicky had created
- Defending decisions that made no sense
- Adopting Vicky's language about "energy" and "alignment."
- Doing more work to avoid them talking together to avoid the conflict

Looking back, I can see how Vicky orchestrated the whole thing. Beth wasn't crazy or difficult – she was just calling out things that didn't make sense. But Vicky needed her gone because truth-tellers are dangerous to people living in lies.

This is how they create their perfect environment: anyone who might question them gets subtly pushed out, while those who play along get rewarded with special status in their "inner circle."

Quiet Guilt-Tripping: The Silent Weapon

IF MANIPULATION IS the sword in their arsenal, guilt-tripping is their stealth bomber. It's so quiet you don't even know you've been hit until you're lying awake at 3 AM wondering why you feel terrible about taking a day off.

Here's how it typically unfolds:

The Martyr Sigh: "No, no, you go home to your family... I'll just finish up here..." (long sigh) "Don't worry about me, I'll figure out how to handle all this somehow..." "Oh, you're taking a vacation? How wonderful..." (distant look) "I can't remember my last real break..." (I personally have done this after being triggered, so don't feel like you are a narcissist for doing some of these things in defense to the actual narcissist)

The Subtle Comparison: "It must be nice to have boundaries..." "Some of us just feel called to give more..." "I wish I could put myself first like that..."

The Implied Disappointment: "I thought you understood our mission here..." "I guess I expected too much..." "Oh... I see where your priorities are..."

And my personal favorite – the Triple Combo:

1. They create an impossible situation.
2. You set a reasonable boundary.
3. They respond with: "I understand completely... I just thought we were the kind of friends/partners/colleagues who..." (trails off meaningfully).

The genius part? None of these are outright accusations. They're more like emotional paper cuts – small enough to make you feel silly for complaining about them but deep enough to leave a mark.

And if you do call them out? "I was just expressing my feelings... why are you so defensive?" This is a classic response from a covert narcissist when they're confronted. In the next chapter, we'll discuss strategies for responding to these behaviors and setting healthy boundaries in your relationships.

Here are a few more examples:

Picture Taylor and Mark's relationship. Everyone thought they were the perfect couple—constantly posting fun adventures, intimate moments, and inside jokes that made others wish they had that connection. Mark made everyone feel special as if they were part of some magical inner circle. However, behind the scenes, Mark was subtly manipulating Taylor into doing things his way, guilt-tripping her when she wanted to spend time with her friends, and gaslighting her into doubting her own feelings.

But watch how the guilt-tripping played out behind the scenes:

When Taylor wanted to visit her family: "Of course you should see them... I get so lonely when you're gone..." "Your sister never really liked me anyway..." "I was hoping we could have one of our special weekends, but family comes first..." (cue sad eyes)

The isolation happened so slowly: "Your mom seems really stressed lately... maybe we should give her space..." "Your friends seem different since we got together... like they're jealous of what we have..." "We don't need anyone else... our connection is so rare..."

The guilt trips became more sophisticated: "Remember how much fun we had last weekend? I miss that closeness when you're with them..." "I just want to protect what we have... nobody understands us like we understand each other..." "I gave up so much to be with you... I thought you'd do the same..."

And here's where guilt-tripping starts dancing with gaslighting: When Taylor questions these patterns, Mark flips the script: "I'm just expressing my love. "Why are you turning our special connection into something negative?" "Maybe your family is the one manipulating you."

The really confusing part? There were magical moments, funny inside jokes, and a special connection. That makes this so effective—not everything is a lie. Some of the intimacy is real, making it harder to spot when it becomes a weapon.

Speaking of weapons, let's talk about their most powerful one – gaslighting. Because once they've got you isolated and feeling guilty about every boundary, that's when they really start making you question your own reality...

Let's look at how Olivia's coworker James mastered the art of making everyone question their reality without ever raising his voice:

The Memory Game: "Oh, we definitely discussed this last month..." (they never did) "I remember you specifically saying you were comfortable with this..." (she never was) "Didn't we agree you'd handle all these tasks?" (they never agreed)

But here's the brilliant part – he'd always add: "But maybe I'm remembering it wrong... I've been so overwhelmed lately..." "It's possible I misunderstood... I was really focused on supporting the team..."

See how he builds in deniability while still planting those seeds of doubt?

The Reality Twist: During team meetings, he'd do something fascinating:

- Olivia would make a point.
- James would rephrase it as his own idea 10 minutes later.
- When Olivia mentioned it was her idea, he'd say gently: "I think you might be confused... we were all building on each other's thoughts..." "Are you feeling okay? You seem really focused on credit lately..."

The Emotional Flip: This is where it gets really sophisticated. When Olivia gets understandably frustrated: "I'm concerned about your emotional state..." "We all notice you've been more sensitive lately..." "Maybe you need time to process whatever you're going through..."

The team started seeing Olivia as "unstable," while James remained calm and supportive, "just trying to help."

But the absolute mastery? The fun times. The team had happy hours when he was charming and inclusive. There were moments of seeming vulnerability when he shared personal struggles. There were times when he publicly praised Olivia (always for trivial things, never for her actual achievements).

These positive moments served two purposes:

1. They made Olivia doubt her growing concerns
2. They made everyone else think she was crazy for having them

The Delegation of Difficult Conversations: "I'm really uncomfortable with conflict. Could you talk to Steve about the missed deadline?" Later, they say, "I can't believe you approached it that way... that's not what we discussed at all."

Or better yet: "Can you let Mandy know about the changes? You're so good at delivering feedback..." Then to Mandy: "I had no idea it would be handled so aggressively. That wasn't my intention at all..."

The Affectionate Put-Downs: "There goes our little perfectionist again!" (pat on the head) "Aww, you're so cute when you get all organized..." "We all know how... particular... you can be about these things..."

Each comment is designed to minimize you while seeming playful. Try to object? "Can't you take a joke? I'm just showing my love!"

The Logic Pretzel: You: "Can you just send me the client report by Friday?" Them: "Why are you so rigid about deadlines?" You: "We discussed this last week..." Them: "I'm feeling really attacked right now..." You: "It's just a simple request..." Them: "This is exactly why I have trouble being creative..."

The Chaos Carousel: Monday: Amazing meeting. Detailed plans were made, and everything was agreed upon. Thursday: "Did we talk about that? I remember it differently..." Friday: "You're being really pushy about this..." Following Monday: "I never said I'd do that... and why are you bringing this up now?"

The Selective Memory Master Class: Covert narcissist says, "Let me tell you what you said in the March meeting. You said my work 'could use improvement' - I remember every word because it was so wounding. In fact, it was March 15th, 2:15 PM, conference room B." Yet the next day, when asked about the report, they promised to complete it: "What report? I don't remember agreeing to anything." When shown the meeting minutes from Monday: "Oh, that meeting? No, I'm sure we were talking about something else entirely." This behavior of a covert narcissist, particularly in a professional setting, is of utmost importance to understand and address because this happens all of the time and is crazy making.

"The Reality Check Scramble: You: "Last week we agreed..." Them: "Did we? I was under so much stress last week..." You: "It was a two-hour conversation..." Them: "Maybe that's how you remember it..." You: "I took notes..." Them: "It concerns me that you feel the need to document everything..."

And the coup de grâce —they'll tell others how "worried" they are about your "memory issues" or your "need for control," setting up a narrative in which your very reasonable requests seem like symptoms of a problem.

What is the most insidious part about all these gaslighting techniques? They work together like a well-orchestrated symphony. The "playful" put-downs soften you up for the reality twisting. Selective memory primes you for self-doubt. The chaos keeps you too off-balance to trust your instincts.

Remember: You're not crazy for documenting conversations, paranoid for double-checking agreements, or "too sensitive" for noticing patterns. Your need for clarity isn't a character flaw—it's your internal warning system trying to break through their fog.

But here's the thing – by the time you're experiencing this level of gaslighting, you're already deep in their web. Which brings us to perhaps the most critical question: How do we spot these patterns before we're caught in them?

In the next chapter, we'll talk about those early warning signs that we usually dismiss with "Oh, they're just being nice" or "They're probably just having a bad day." We'll explore why love-bombing doesn't always look like grand gestures (sometimes it's just a whisper), how boundary violations can be so subtle you don't notice them until it's too late, and why that cycle of devaluation often feels like constructive feedback at first.

Because here's the truth: Covert narcissists don't start with blatant manipulation. They start with something much more subtle – you feel like you are finally being seen, understood, and appreciated...

Chapter 3: Check the Board - Early Signs of Danger

You know that feeling when you walk into a room, and the air feels different? Not obviously wrong, just... off? That's precisely what the initial stages of involvement with a covert narcissist feel like. Everything seems perfect – maybe too perfect – but something in your gut is trying to tell you something.

Early warning signs are easy to miss, especially when you're being love-bombed with a whisper instead of a shout. Picture this: You meet someone who seems to... get you. Really get you. They mirror your interests, values, and dreams. It feels magical.

They share eerily similar life experiences: "Oh my god, I went through exactly the same thing!" They position themselves as your perfect confidante: "I feel like I've known you forever." They create an insider status: "Not everyone gets this like we do."

The Magnetic Pull

IT STARTS LIKE A DREAM collaboration. Unlike obvious love-bombing with grand gestures, this is more subtle—like being pulled into the most exciting creative partnership of your life. The team dynamic feels electric. You finish each other's sentences, building on each other's ideas. They seem to amplify your light and reflect your brilliance. But watch carefully—they're not just mirroring; they're studying, learning, and absorbing.

Then comes their problem person – maybe a former business partner, an ex-friend, or a difficult family member. The stories initially seem reasonable: "They just couldn't handle authentic communication." "They were threatened by our connection." These conversations never end and always circle back to the same person, testing your loyalty and gauging your boundaries.

The Energy Drain

WHILE YOU'RE POURING out your expertise, passion, and ideas, they're taking notes. They learn your language, absorb your practices, and study your approaches. Soon, they're using your phrases, adopting your practices (but claiming they're "naturally gifted"), and positioning themselves as the source of wisdom you shared.

The boundary erosion happens so subtly. "Can you just look at this quick email?" "Would you mind sharing your contact list? We're in this together." Each request seems reasonable in isolation. But quick favors become expectations. Your resources become "our" resources. Your boundaries become "resistance to the vision."

Watch how they test limits—late-night texts about "inspiration," emergencies requiring immediate attention, and plans that overlap with your personal commitments. If you protest, "I thought we were aligned in this." "Your boundaries feel like walls to me." Yet their personal commitments always take precedence.

They gradually claim ownership of everything: your ideas become "when we came up with," your connections become "our friend from the conference," and your methods become "the way we do things."

The Human Response

HERE'S WHAT NOBODY talks about: what happens when perfectly stable people start acting "crazy" in response to crazy-making behavior. After months or years of ignoring boundaries, watching someone take credit for your work, being subtly undermined, and having reality twisted, you might find yourself sending that angry text at 2 AM or finally exploding in a meeting.

The genuinely diabolical part? They feed off both positive and negative energy. Your frustration fuels their "concerned" narrative. Your success fuels their ability to take credit. They float through meetings looking perfectly composed while you're exhausted from doing all the actual work and managing their chaos.

When you finally hit your limit and walk away, they play the victim while you look unstable. Your silence (out of integrity) protects their image, and their inner circle never knows the truth. Because while you were trying to be loyal and professional, they were crafting their narrative of your "instability" and their "patience."

This is the covert narcissist's game - subtle, sophisticated, and devastating in its effectiveness.

Being depleted by a covert narcissist feels different from normal tiredness. It's a soul-deep exhaustion that creeps up so gradually you might not notice until you're running on empty.

Think about how you feel after interactions with them - not just tired, but bizarrely responsible for their emotions. Your successes somehow become part of their story. Your energy gets drained while they seem mysteriously energized. You find yourself doing more and more while they do less and less.

The pattern is insidious. They come to you "desperate" for help or guidance. You pour your energy into helping them. They walk away revitalized while you feel depleted. Then, they take your ideas, work, and energy into other relationships. When you start to pull back, they return needing another "fix."

What's truly maddening is watching them use what they've taken from you. They use your expertise while claiming ignorance, need your help while appearing self-sufficient, drain your energy while looking energized, and take credit while playing humble.

They maintain multiple sources of supply—at work, in friendships, through social media, and in romantic relationships. They always keep backup people in orbit, ready to step in when one source runs dry. It's like watching someone perform a show using your script, your stage directions, and your choreography while you stand exhausted in the wings.

And when do you start noticing this pattern? When you begin pulling back? That's when they create a crisis that needs your attention, love-bomb you back into the pattern, remind you of your "special connection," or make you feel guilty for "abandoning" them.

The awakening comes when you realize that this isn't a partnership. It's not even a one-way street. It's an energy harvest, and you're the crop.

The Slow Slide into Devaluation

LET ME TELL YOU ABOUT Shelly's last few months running her wellness center with her business partner, Emily. It started with small things:

"You're so amazing at handling all the details while I focus on our vision!" (Translation: I'm dumping all the work on you but making it sound like a compliment)

Then came the strategic absences: "I know it's our busiest season, but I need this spiritual retreat. You're so good at managing everything... it's just two weeks!" Two weeks turned into three, then four. Meanwhile, Shelly was juggling client loads, managing staff, and keeping the business afloat.

When Emily returned, glowing and refreshed, her promise to take over the bookkeeping mysteriously vanished. "Oh, you've got such a great system going now... it would be silly to change it!" Never mind that Shelly was working until midnight doing both their jobs.

The devaluation really kicks in when you start questioning these patterns. Watch how it unfolds:

Week 1: You mention the broken promises: "I need space to process this..." (Disappears for days while you keep everything running)

Week 2: You try to set boundaries. "I'm feeling really attacked right now..." (Still not handling their responsibilities)

Week 3: You express frustration: "You've changed... you used to be so understanding..." (Meanwhile, you're still carrying their workload)

And here's the genius part: While you're becoming increasingly frustrated (because who wouldn't be?), they're crafting their masterpiece. They tell others how "worried" they are about you, carefully documenting your "emotional" responses. Every interaction becomes part of their narrative about your "negativity," while they ensure everyone witnesses their infinite "patience."

The final twist of the knife? By the time you hit your limit, they've already laid their groundwork. They've created a story about your "instability" and positioned themselves as the rational, concerned friend. They've gathered sympathy from others about how "hard" it's been dealing with your decline. So, when you finally break, it looks like it came out of nowhere - just as they planned.

This is their art - making your natural reaction to their manipulation look like evidence of your instability. When you realize what's happening, the narrative is already written, and you're cast as the unstable one in their carefully crafted story.

They discard you while making it look like you're the one who couldn't handle the relationship. All those months or years of keeping quiet about their behavior, trying to be professional, not wanting to bad-mouth them? That silence gets used against you because no one saw the slow erosion that led to your final breaking point. Then, if you go low contact or have no contact, they let everyone think you abandoned them out of the blue. People see you as the villain, and there are no words to fight this, so it is a no-win situation.

These patterns of early warning signs, love-bombing whispers, boundary violations, and devaluation aren't random – they're the carefully laid foundation for something much more comprehensive: a web of control so subtle you won't realize you're caught in it until you try to move.

Because here's the truth: All those early red flags, seemingly small boundary crosses, and moments of devaluation are just the preparation for the real trap. They're testing how much you'll tolerate, how deeply they can sink their hooks in, and how thoroughly they can weave their web around your life.

In the next chapter, we'll explore exactly how they build this web of control. We'll look at how they create financial dependencies so subtle you might not notice them until you try to leave. We'll examine their masterful social isolation tactics that make you feel simultaneously surrounded by people and completely alone. And perhaps most importantly, we'll understand the trauma bond trap – that powerful psychological chain that keeps you tied to someone who's hurting you while making you believe they're helping.

Because understanding how this web is woven is the first step to finding your way out of it...

Chapter 4: Spinning the Web in the Game of Control

Have you ever watched a spider build its web? It doesn't start in the middle. It begins with those outer support strands – the ones you might not notice until you walk right into them. That's precisely how covert narcissists build their web of control.

Financial Strings

LET ME TELL YOU ABOUT Rhonda and her "collaborative" business partnership. It started innocently: "Let's keep our finances fluid since we're building this together..." "Why don't you just cover this expense? I'll get the next one..." "It makes more sense if you handle the invoicing since you're so organized..."

Three years later, Rhonda realized:

- All the business expenses were on her credit cards
- Her partner's name wasn't on any of the loans
- The biggest clients were somehow personally connected to her partner
- She did 80% of the work, but everything was "shared equally."

Or take Michael's marriage to Samantha: "I'm just not good with money... you're so much better at it..." "Since you're handling the finances, I'll focus on making our house beautiful..." "Don't worry about my spending – look how much value I add to our life!"

The trap? By the time Michael realized Samantha had run up massive debt in his name, she had:

- Access to all his accounts
- Control of their public image
- A story about his "controlling behavior" with money
- A network of people who believed her version

Here's the real genius: They create financial entanglements while appearing to be either helpless with money or trustworthy. There's no middle ground. They're either:

- Too incompetent to handle money (so you must do it)
- Or so skilled you should trust them completely

The Financial Power Play

CONSIDER AMANDA AND Heather's business partnership. Amanda had a fascinating approach to their shared finances:

When it was her idea: "We simply must invest in this retreat - it's for our growth!" "This designer website is crucial for our brand." "Of course, we must take the whole team out for this celebration."

But when Heather suggested spending: "Is this really necessary right now?" "We should be more conservative with our resources." "Maybe we can find a cheaper alternative..."

The real power move? Amanda would make these pronouncements in front of their team: "Heather, can you hold off on ordering those supplies? We need to be careful with spending..." (Meanwhile, Amanda had just booked a $ 5,000' team building' event).

The Social Power Dance

THIS FINANCIAL CONTROL wove perfectly into social control. Take Shelly and Emily's "equal" partnership at their event company. Emily had mastered the art of public power plays:

In team meetings: "Shelly, honey, can you handle all the follow-up calls? You're so good with details..." (Said with a sweet smile that dared Shelly to object in front of everyone)

To clients: "We do things a certain way here, right Shelly?" (The subtle emphasis makes it clear who really set the rules)

The isolation was masterful because it happened in plain sight. Emily created an inner circle in which Shelly found herself in an impossible position—included just enough to seem favored yet excluded enough to feel powerless. She was visible enough that others saw her as "in," yet controlled enough that she couldn't speak up without consequences.

If Shelly tried to object to anything, Emily had positioned herself so perfectly that every response would backfire. The team would see Shelly as difficult, clients would view her as unprofessional, and their social circle would dismiss her as jealous. The inner circle, Emily's carefully cultivated audience, would begin their subtle freeze-out.

The real trap? Shelly understood the cost of speaking up. She knew she'd lose professional connections, be labeled as dramatic, and get pushed out of their social sphere. Any attempt to address the situation would just make her look like she was playing the victim. Emily had created a perfect prison of perception—one where Shelly's attempts to free herself would only tighten the bars.

This is how covert narcissists keep control - not through apparent force, but through careful social choreography where every move their target makes plays right into their narrative.

And Emily knew it, too. She could say things like: "Shelly, dear, I've already decided we're doing it this way" in front of others, knowing Shelly would smile and go along to avoid looking like the difficult one.

The Trauma Bond Trap

FIRST, LET'S UNDERSTAND what 'trauma bonding' actually is. It's like being tied to someone with a rope made of hope, fear, guilt, and moments of pure magic. This bond forms when the person who hurts you is also the one you turn to for comfort from that very pain. It's a complex emotional connection that keeps you tied to someone who's not good for you.

Consider Ashley and Mike's dynamic: Monday: Mike publicly undermines Ashley in a team meeting. Tuesday: Mike brings her favorite coffee and tells her how special she is. Wednesday: Mike 'forgets' a vital commitment, leaving her scrambling. Thursday: Mike shows up with emotional support when she's stressed. Friday: Mike takes credit for her work. Weekend: Mike plans something magical that reminds her of their early days. This cycle of hurt and comfort is a classic example of trauma bonding.

The cycle creates a potent chemical cocktail in your brain that hooks you deeper with each round. The stress floods your system with cortisol, while those make-up moments release waves of oxytocin. You live in constant anticipation, triggering dopamine hits, while walking on eggshells keeps your adrenaline flowing. It's a perfect storm of addiction - your brain literally becomes hooked on the cycle, leaving you in a state of emotional turmoil.

Like a gambler at a slot machine, you keep pulling the lever, hoping for those magical moments to return. The trauma bond deepens as they position themselves as both the source of your pain and your only comfort. They understand the pressure you're under (that they created), offer comfort for the pain they caused, and create problems only to 'help' you solve them. They become your safe harbor in the chaos they generate. It's the perfect con - they're selling you both the poison and the antidote, a clear example of psychological manipulation.

The most confusing part is when they suddenly vanish. One day, you're planning the future together, the next day... silence. Take Jamie's experience with her business partner, Lexi. They were deep into their biggest project when suddenly Lexi stopped responding to texts. Meetings got canceled at the last minute. Everything felt... off. There was no explanation, just absence.

You know that sick feeling? The one where you're scrolling through recent conversations, trying to figure out what you did wrong? That's the trauma bond, speaking. Because here's what happens next - Lexi reappears like nothing happened: "Oh my god, I missed you so much! You won't believe what I've been going through..."

And just like that, you're pulled back in. Because now they need you. They've got a crisis only you can understand, a drama that explains everything, a special connection that needs rekindling, a future that looks bright again. The cycle begins anew, each turn binding you tighter to their reality.

The really crazy-making part? When you start feeling secure again, they'll disappear once more. It's like emotional whiplash. One minute, you're their person, rock, and special one. The next minute... ghost town.

And every time they return, the story gets better: "You're the only one who truly gets me..." "I've been doing so much healing work..." "I am so sorry I went MIA, but things will be different now..."

Here's what makes trauma bonding so powerful - they're hurting you and healing you at the same time. They're the person who abandons you AND the only one who can make it better.

Let me show you how this cycle of abandonment and return gets more intense, like waves getting bigger in a storm:

Picture this: You're finally getting your feet under you after their last disappearing act. You've almost convinced yourself you're okay with the silence. Then suddenly - ping! A text at 2 AM:

"Been thinking about you. I want to say I had a vision about you, and I love you..."

And just like that, you're wide awake, heart pounding. Because they know exactly what to say: "Nobody understood our vision like we did..." "Remember how magical those early days were?" "I've been doing so much work on myself..."

The returns become more dramatic each time. Bigger promises, deeper insights, more convincing explanations—like my friend Kate's business partner, who vanished for three weeks and then showed up with: "The universe was testing our bond..." "I had to go on that trip, or I would have never heard the end of it..." "This was all part of our growth..."

Meanwhile, you're living in a constant state of:

- Waiting for the other shoe to drop
- Walking on eggshells to keep them around
- Trying to prove your loyalty
- Hoping this time will be different

Each cycle makes you more desperate to keep them close, more willing to accept the unacceptable, and more ready to ignore your gut feelings. Because the alternative - losing that magical connection again feels heart-wrenching, and all of the responsibilities are tied together.

And here's the genuinely devastating part: While you're going through emotional hell during their absences, they're often:

- Living their best life
- Creating new connections
- Building other relationships
- Planning their next return

And here's why this web of control is so hard to break free from—by the time you realize what's happening, everything is entangled. It's not just about emotions anymore—it's about real life, with all its complicated connections.

In romantic relationships, you share a home you both love, friend groups who see you as a unit, financial commitments, and dreams you've built together. Maybe there are children involved who need stability or family ties that have grown deep on both sides.

In business partnerships, you've created something real—loyal customers who trust both of you, a brand that means something, and staff who depend on their paychecks. There are contracts, relationships, and years of built-up goodwill that can't just be undone overnight.

This isn't about being weak or desperate. Let me say that again—this is NOT about being weak. In fact, it's often the strongest people who stay the longest, trying to make things work, believing in the potential of others, and honoring their commitments. Empaths especially tend to be incredibly resilient people who can handle more than most—that's part of why we end up in these situations.

Yes, I was a martyr in my situation. Maybe you're a perfectionist in yours. We all have our patterns we're working on. But here's the difference - we can acknowledge our flaws while still trying to grow. Covert narcissists use their "flaws" as weapons while refusing to change.

The web they weave isn't just sticky—it's structural. Everything is connected. That's why untangling ourselves takes time, strategy, and support. We're not just trying to break free—we're trying to do it without destroying everything and everyone we care about in the process.

Remember: Your compassion isn't weakness, your hope isn't naivety, and your commitment isn't foolishness. These are beautiful qualities that someone has twisted into chains.

The web of control we've been discussing leaves more than just external tangles - it creates deep internal wounds that can be hard to recognize while you're still caught in them. Let's talk about what happens to us when we've been dancing with a covert narcissist for months, years, or even decades.

Chapter 5: Stuck in the Game – The Emotional Price

You know that feeling when you catch yourself in the mirror and barely recognize who's looking back? Or when you find yourself apologizing for things that aren't your fault? Or lying awake at 3 AM wondering how you got here? That's what we need to talk about.

The impact of covert narcissistic abuse isn't always as visible as a bruise. It's more like a slow erosion of your sense of reality, confidence, and health. Let's start by understanding why we often feel like we're losing our minds - that mental tug-of-war called cognitive dissonance.

Because here's the truth: Before we can heal, we need to understand what we're healing from. And sometimes, the most complex wounds to heal are the ones we can't see.

Cognitive Dissonance: When Your Heart and Head Are at War

PICTURE THIS: YOU'RE sitting in a meeting watching your business partner take credit for your work - again. They're telling the story of "their" brilliant idea (the one you stayed up all night developing), and they're doing it with such conviction that, for a moment, you actually question your own memory. Are you remembering it wrong? They may have come up with it.

Or you're watching your partner charm everyone at a family gathering, being thoughtful and attentive, and thinking, "Maybe I'm the problem. They're so wonderful with everyone else. Maybe I'm too sensitive, too demanding, too... much."

This is cognitive dissonance - a maddening space between what you know and what you're being told to believe. It's like living in two realities at once, a constant struggle that many of us have experienced:

Reality One: They're taking advantage of you. You have the receipts, the texts, the sleepless nights, the empty promises.

Reality Two: They're so giving, so special, so misunderstood. Look how they just helped that stranger! Look how everyone else loves them!

Your mind tries desperately to bridge these two realities. Maybe they're stressed. Perhaps if you were more understanding? Maybe if you tried harder? Maybe, maybe...

This constant mental gymnastics exhausts you, as you're trying to make sense of things that don't make sense. You're trying to write a logical story about an illogical situation. And the worst part? The longer this goes on, the more you stop trusting your own judgment.

Trauma Responses: When Fight, Flight, or Freeze Takes Over

LET ME TELL YOU ABOUT Lilly and the ripple effect of covert narcissism. Twenty years ago, while studying psychology in college, I saw something I didn't fully understand until years later. Lilly was a close friend of mine, and we often discussed our studies and personal experiences with psychology. She had what seemed like a troubled marriage. She constantly talked about her husband's 'angry outbursts' and 'unstable behavior.' She had a way of sharing these stories that made everyone sympathize with her while painting him as the villain.

But here's what I noticed: Lilly had this group of devoted friends - what we call 'flying monkeys' in narcissistic abuse dynamics. These are people who are the covert narcissist's allies, often recruited (sometimes without them even realizing it) to carry out their agenda, spread their narrative, and reinforce their version of reality. Lilly's flying monkeys would rally around her, confirm her stories, and help spread the word about her husband's difficulty. They were unwitting pawns in the narcissist's game, manipulated into believing and supporting the narcissist's version of events.

Looking back now, after experiencing my own encounter with Lilly's manipulation during my internship, I see something different. Her husband's "angry outbursts" were likely trauma responses to years of subtle manipulation, gaslighting, and emotional abuse. Think about it - he was:

- Constantly being discussed behind his back
- Having his reactions scrutinized and reported to others
- Trying to maintain stability for their kids
- Watching his reputation being slowly destroyed
- Living with someone who appeared perfect to the outside world while slowly driving him crazy at home

When someone is subjected to this kind of ongoing covert abuse, they often develop trauma responses that make them look like the "crazy" ones.

These responses can manifest in various ways, such as becoming controlling because they feel so out of control, acting paranoid because their reality is constantly being questioned, and lashing out because they're drowning in confusion and frustration. Other responses might include withdrawing from social interactions, experiencing panic attacks, or developing physical symptoms like headaches or stomach issues.

And here's the masterful part - the covert narcissist then uses these very responses as proof of their original narrative. "See? I told you he was unstable. I told you he was angry. I told you I was the victim."

Let me explain how these trauma responses spiral into deeper health issues:

When your body and mind are constantly on high alert, things start to break down. I watched this happen with Lilly's husband and later recognized it in myself and others who've dealt with covert narcissists. The constant state of confusion and defense doesn't just affect your emotions - it changes your whole system.

Think about living in a state where your stomach is always in knots because you never know when the next subtle attack is coming. Your sleep is disrupted because your mind keeps replaying conversations, looking for where you went wrong. Your appetite either disappears or becomes your only comfort. Your jaw stays clenched from holding back what you really want to say.

The erosion of self-worth is like a slow-dripping faucet. Each drop might seem small: "Maybe I am too sensitive..." "I should be more understanding..." "If I were stronger/better/smarter, I could handle this..."

Until one day, you wake up and realize you've lost yourself completely.

I saw this with my own trauma response to Lilly during my internship. Even though I was studying psychology, even though I should have "known better," I found myself:

- Second-guessing my professional judgment
- Apologizing for having boundaries
- Feeling crazy for noticing inconsistencies
- Doubting my own memories of events

And here's what makes this so insidious - these responses don't go away when the relationship ends. They become part of your operating system. Years later, in entirely different situations, you might find yourself:

- Flinching at subtle criticism
- Overexplaining your decisions
- Apologizing for having needs
- Bracing for abandonment

This is how the damage compounds - not just in the moment, but in how it changes how we move through the world.

Let me explain how this constant state of stress and trauma literally rewires our body and brain:

The Physical Toll of Covert Abuse:

Your body keeps the score long before your mind understands what's happening. That constant state of anticipating the next subtle dig, the next disappearing act, the next guilt trip - it takes a devastating physical toll.

Think about what happens to your body when you're in this constant state of alert: Your heart starts doing that flutter-skip dance (those aren't butterflies; they're stress palpitations). Your skin starts crawling or itching for no apparent reason. Your brain feels wrapped in cotton, like fog, where you can't quite grasp thoughts. Your cortisol levels stay sky-high, leading to weight gain around your middle, and your vagus nerve - that superhighway of calm - gets squeezed into constant fight-or-flight mode.

I remember sitting in my doctor's office, trying to explain these symptoms: "No, I'm not in an abusive relationship... they're actually really supportive... I'm probably just working too hard..."

Meanwhile, my body was screaming what my mind couldn't accept: mysterious digestive issues, chronic tension headaches, insomnia, or exhaustion (sometimes both), random body aches, and that tight band around your chest that never entirely goes away.

And here's what's really messed up - your nervous system gets so used to chaos that calm feels wrong. You find yourself unable to relax even when things are good, waiting for the other shoe to drop, feeling more anxious when things are peaceful, and creating drama because quiet feels threatening.

Your brain's alarm system is stuck in the 'on' position, and your body pays the price. Those neural pathways have been carved so deeply that your body remembers them after the relationship ends. It's not just emotional baggage - it's physical rewiring that needs to be healed.

After months or years of covert narcissistic abuse, your body and mind start sending clear distress signals. Here's what that looks like:

Physical Symptoms:

- Heart palpitations and chest tightness
- Chronic digestive issues and IBS
- Tension headaches and migraines
- Brain fog and memory issues
- Autoimmune flare-ups
- Chronic fatigue but unable to rest
- Hair loss and skin problems
- Tight jaw and dental issues
- High blood pressure
- Weight gain or loss
- Thyroid dysfunction
- Adrenal fatigue

Mental and Emotional Impact:

- Constant anxiety and hypervigilance
- Depression that comes in waves
- Memory gaps and confusion

- Difficulty making simple decisions
- Emotional numbness alternating with overwhelming feelings
- Inability to trust your own judgment
- Persistent self-doubt
- Fear of abandonment
- Panic attacks
- Insomnia or vivid nightmares
- Dissociation
- Complex PTSD symptoms

The real kicker? While you're experiencing all of this, the covert narcissist often appears to be thriving. They're getting compliments on how well they're handling things while you look "unstable" or "not coping well."

And here's what many people don't understand: These aren't just temporary stress responses. This kind of prolonged trauma actually changes your brain chemistry. Your nervous system gets rewired for danger. Your body forgets how to feel safe.

The healing journey isn't just about getting away from them - it's about literally rebuilding your neural pathways, resetting your nervous system, and teaching your body it's safe to relax again.

Recognizing Symptoms as Signals, Not Failures

WHEN YOUR BODY AND mind are screaming through symptoms, it's not weakness - it's wisdom. Your system is telling you something important. Instead of pushing through or beating yourself up, let's look at how to listen and heal.

The Path to Nervous System Recovery

FIRST, UNDERSTAND THAT healing from covert narcissistic abuse requires a multi-faceted approach. Your nervous system has been through a war - it needs gentle, consistent care to find its way back to balance.

Consider this healing toolkit:

Somatic (Body-Based) Healing: Massage isn't just a luxury—it's medicine for your overwhelmed nervous system. It helps release trauma stored in your tissues. Regular bodywork can also help your vagus nerve remember how to relax.

Breathing and Meditation: Simple box breathing can interrupt the panic cycle. Meditation, even just five minutes daily, helps rebuild those neural pathways of safety. Your breath is always with you - it's your portable peace tool.

Light Therapy and Sensory Healing: Our bodies crave light and rhythm. Light therapy can help reset your circadian rhythms after they've been disrupted by constant stress. Some people find that infrared saunas help release the physical tension of trauma.

Professional Support: Traditional talk therapy is excellent, but for this kind of trauma, consider the following:

- Gestalt therapy to reconnect with your authentic self
- EMDR to process traumatic memories
- Hypnosis to reprogram those stress responses
- Somatic experiencing to release trapped trauma

Spiritual Connection: Whether it's prayer, nature walks, or quiet contemplation - finding your spiritual center can provide an anchor when everything else feels chaotic. This isn't about any particular religion - it's about connecting to something more significant than the trauma.

Remember: Healing isn't linear. Some days, you'll feel stronger, and others, you might need to cocoon. Listen to your body—it's been through enough ignoring.

The impact of covert narcissistic abuse runs deep - through our bodies, minds, and spirits. But understanding these effects is the first step toward healing them. When we recognize that our symptoms aren't character flaws but rather normal responses to abnormal situations, we can start being gentler with ourselves.

Your body has been keeping score; now it's time to help it heal. Healing is possible through bodywork, therapy, spiritual practice, or a combination of many approaches. The same sensitivity that made you vulnerable to a covert narcissist is also your superpower in recovery—your ability to feel deeply means you can heal deeply, too.

But before we dive into recovery, we need to talk about how to break free. Understanding the impact is only part of the journey. Next, we need to look at how to actually break the spell they've cast—how to recognize your reality, document the abuse, build your support network, and develop an escape plan that keeps you safe.

Breaking the spell will show you exactly how to start untangling yourself from their web, one thread at a time...

Chapter 6: Checkmate Reversed – Escaping the Narcissist's Play

There comes a moment when something shifts. Maybe it's small - they make a subtle dig that finally doesn't land. Perhaps it's big - you catch them in a lie they can't talk their way out of. But something clicks, and suddenly, you start seeing the pattern. That's when the real work begins.

Let's discuss the most powerful word in your new vocabulary: No.

It's just two letters, but to a covert narcissist, it's kryptonite. "No, that doesn't work for me." "No, I won't be available." "No, I don't remember it that way." Simple, direct, decisive. This is your power, your control, your empowerment.

But before you can start saying no, you must be rock-solid in your reality. Because they're masters at making you doubt yourself, making you feel crazy for setting boundaries and questioning your memories.

Recognizing Your Reality

FIRST, LET'S DISCUSS what's really happening versus what they want you to think is happening. Their power lies in keeping you confused, off balance, and second-guessing yourself. Your power lies in seeing things clearly.

When they say, "You're too sensitive," what's happening is you're reacting normally to abnormal behavior.

When they say, "You're imagining things," what's really happening is you're noticing patterns they don't want you to see.

When they say, "You're making too big a deal of this," what's really happening is you're finally standing up for yourself.

Remember: Emotional and psychological abuse can be just as damaging as physical abuse - sometimes more so because the wounds aren't visible, and the tactics are more challenging to prove. But just because you can't show someone a bruise doesn't mean you're not being hurt.

It can take a shocking moment to finally see the truth:

Sometimes, it takes one undeniable moment to shatter the illusion. Let me tell you about Petra's wake-up call.

Petra and Justine were driving to an event when they disagreed - nothing major, just Petra expressing concern about some business decisions. Justine, who had always portrayed herself as caring and spiritually evolved, did something unthinkable: she pulled over and ordered Petra out of the car.

Right there, on a deserted road, knowing full well about Petra's severe anxiety and physical health issues. No phone, no nearby businesses, just... abandoned. Because Petra dared to question her.

That was the moment the mask entirely slipped. All those little incidents Petra had explained away suddenly came into sharp focus. The "spiritual" friend who preached compassion had just left a sick person stranded because she didn't like being challenged.

This is when Petra started documenting everything. Because she knew her mind would try to slip back into denial, make excuses, and minimize what happened. That's what trauma does - it tries to protect us by helping us forget. But some things shouldn't be forgotten.

Here's how to document covert abuse:

Start a reality journal - not just what they do, but how it makes you feel. Include:

- Dates and times
- Exact quotes when possible
- Who else was present
- Your physical reactions (anxiety, nausea, panic)
- Any witnesses or evidence
- Screenshots of texts or emails
- Records of financial transactions
- Broken promises and gaslighting attempts

Most importantly, document the pattern. Because covert narcissists rarely have big, dramatic outbursts. Instead, they create death by a thousand cuts - each small enough to doubt but devastating in their accumulation.

Sometimes, you're not documenting for court—you're documenting for your own sanity. Every time you start to doubt yourself, every time you think, "Maybe I'm overreacting," every time you're tempted to go back to pretending everything's fine, your journal becomes your anchor to reality.

Please keep it simple. Keep it real: "Today, she promised to handle the client presentation. An hour before, she texted that she had forgotten her appointment and that I had to do it. Again."

"He said we never discussed the budget. I know we did. Three times. I have the meeting notes."

Your documentation doesn't have to be perfect. It just has to be true.

Now, about that support network - quality matters more than quantity. You don't need an army. You need a few people who:

- Believe you without requiring proof

- Don't rush to give advice
- Can hold space for your confusion
- Won't push you to "just get over it."
- Understand that healing isn't linear

Sometimes, it's just one solid friend and a good therapist. Sometimes, it's a support group. Sometimes, it's a family member who sees through the mask. Finding people who won't minimize your experience or push you to "fix" things before you're ready is key. You are not alone in this.

Remember: Not everyone needs to understand your story, and not everyone deserves to hear it. Choose your confidants carefully. Some people aren't equipped to handle this kind of truth, and that's okay. This isn't about convincing the world but finding your way back to yourself.

Developing Your Escape Plan

FIRST, UNDERSTAND THIS: Leaving a covert narcissist isn't like ending a normal relationship. You need a strategy because they've woven deeply into your life. And sometimes, the most potent exit is the quietest one. This plan will give you the security and preparation you need.

Your escape plan needs to protect three things:

- Your emotional wellbeing
- Your practical needs
- Your future peace

Start with the practical stuff. Get your documentation in order but keep it somewhere safe - not on shared computers or spaces. If you're in business together, start gathering:

- Contracts and agreements
- Financial records
- Client information
- Important emails
- Creative work

If it's a personal relationship, focus on:

- Personal documents
- Financial information
- Important memories and keepsakes
- Evidence of shared property or agreements

But here's what's really important - don't telegraph your moves. Covert narcissists are experts at 'hoovering' you back in when they sense you're pulling away. 'Hoovering' is a manipulation tactic where they'll suddenly become the person you first fell in love with or went into business with. They'll make promises. They'll show glimpses of insight. It's a ploy to keep you hooked.

Stay strong. Remember: Their moments of self-awareness are usually just another manipulation tool.

Developing Your Escape Plan

SOMETIMES, THE MOST powerful thing you can do is walk away. Let me tell you about John, a mortgage broker who discovered this truth the hard way.

John had built a successful business with his partner Bob. While John handled the daily client needs, marketing campaigns, backend operations, and customer service, Bob was living his best life—traveling to Italy, enjoying Hawaii, going camping, and taking boat trips. Most notably, he made promises he rarely kept.

John tried to do it "the right way for a year." He sent emails requesting specific help, documented the uneven workload, and tried having conversations about fair partnership. The response? Silence—or worse, vague promises that led nowhere.

When John finally took a vacation, something interesting happened. The business started falling apart without him. But instead of this being a "gotcha" moment, it was a revelation: He was carrying the entire load anyway. Why not carry it for himself?

So, John did something radical—he walked away and gave Bob the whole business. On paper, it looked like John lost everything. But what he actually lost was constant anxiety, endless frustration, daily resentment, and the exhaustion of carrying someone else's empty promises. He gained his self-respect, peace of mind, and the ability to be kind again.

John started his own agency, doing the same amount of work but without the constant drain of managing someone else's empty promises. The lesson? Sometimes, the cleanest break is the best break. You don't always need to win the battle to regain your life.

When planning your own exit, consider these three crucial elements:

- Your safety (emotional and physical)
- Your non-negotiables (what you absolutely must keep)
- Your peace of mind (often worth more than material things)

I remember another client, Kelly, who left her thriving yoga studio partnership because her covert narcissistic partner had made it a toxic environment. Everyone thought she was crazy to leave such a "successful" business. But like John, she found that running a smaller studio alone was infinitely more peaceful than managing a bigger one with someone who drained her soul.

The key is to plan your exit quietly, methodically, and with your eyes on the future rather than the past. Document what you need to, gather your support system, and remember - sometimes losing everything is the path to gaining yourself back.

The Aftermath and Different Types of Exits

LEAVING A COVERT NARCISSIST looks different depending on your situation. While John could walk away from his business, leaving a marriage or family situation often requires more careful planning.

Take Mary's story. She knew she needed to leave her marriage, but her husband had slowly taken control of all their finances. She started by squirreling away small amounts of money when grocery shopping, opening a separate bank account at a different bank, and gathering important documents. She made copies of tax returns during tax season when it wouldn't seem suspicious. Her "book club" became her cover for meeting with a divorce attorney.

Or consider Kate's need to distance herself from her covert narcissist mother. She couldn't cut ties - she had young children and family obligations. Instead, she began what she called a "gentle fade": longer times between visits, shorter phone calls, and less sharing of personal information. She developed a technique called "grey rocking with a smile" - being pleasant but increasingly less available.

The key is matching your exit strategy to your situation. A business partner might need careful documentation of intellectual property. A spouse might need a safety deposit box and an escape fund. A family member might need firm boundaries and a support system.

What they all have in common is this: The exit isn't just physical - it's psychological. You're not just leaving a situation; you're reclaiming your reality.

Remember: The goal isn't to win every battle. The goal is to get free with enough of yourself intact to rebuild. Sometimes, that means leaving with less than you deserve materially but with your spirit whole.

Rebuilding After the Storm

THAT FIRST BREATH OF freedom often feels more like suffocation. Whether you've left a business partnership, marriage, or toxic family situation, you might struggle with the most challenging part - the internal war between what you know you had to do and what you wish you could have done.

The decision to go no-contact or low-contact often feels like becoming the very villain they accused you of being. The guilt can be overwhelming: "Maybe I didn't try hard enough..." "What will people think?" "Am I the toxic one for walking away?"

Here's the truth: It often gets worse before it gets better. That cognitive dissonance hits hard when you're alone with your thoughts. You might find yourself missing the very person who hurt you, doubting your memories of the abuse, feeling guilty for "abandoning" them, or questioning if you're overreacting.

Gina, who left her manipulative business partner, spent the first month feeling like she was having a breakdown. "I felt worse after leaving than I did in the relationship," she told me. "I kept thinking maybe I was the problem. Maybe I was too sensitive. Maybe I should have tried harder."

This is normal. Your brain is literally rewiring itself, breaking free from the trauma bonds. The confusion isn't a sign you made the wrong choice - it's proof of how deep the manipulation went.

The guilt of being the "bad guy" can be incredibly intense when others don't understand your decision. Family members might pressure you to reconcile. Mutual friends might think you're overreacting. The covert narcissist might be playing the victim beautifully.

Remember: Healing isn't linear. Some days, you'll feel strong and confident. On other days, you'll want to call them and apologize for leaving. Both reactions are part of the process.

What helps during this time:

- A therapist who understands narcissistic abuse
- A solid support person who won't judge your confusion
- Permission to feel everything without acting on it
- Reminders of why you left (this is where your documentation helps)

The art of rebuilding requires a delicate balance. While it's healthy—even necessary—to spend time alone processing your experience, complete isolation can become a trap. There's a difference between peaceful solitude and lonely isolation.

Some alone time helps you:

- Hear your own thoughts again
- Process your feelings without interference
- Rediscover your own preferences
- Rest your nervous system

But we also need connection. Maybe it's just one trusted friend who gets it. It could be a support group. Perhaps it's a therapist. Finding people who can hold space for your healing without rushing you through it is key.

Self-care becomes critical during this time. Not just the bubble baths and meditation apps (though those can help), but the deep self-care of:

- Setting boundaries without guilt
- Saying no when you need to
- Resting when you're tired
- Eating when you're hungry
- Moving your body gently
- Being kind to yourself when the guilt hits

Remember: You're not just healing from what happened - you're healing from who you had to become to survive. That takes time, patience, and tremendous self-compassion.

The journey of breaking free from a covert narcissist isn't just about making an exit plan - it's about reclaiming your power, one small decision at a time. Whether you're leaving a business partnership like John, a marriage like Gina, or a toxic family situation like Kate, remember this: Your exit doesn't have to be perfect to be powerful. You don't have to win every battle to win your freedom. Sometimes, the quietest exits create the loudest impact in your life.

As we move into the next chapter about handling the immediate aftermath, remember that breaking the spell is just the beginning. The real work and healing often start in those first raw days and weeks after you've made your break. Your documentation will help you stay strong, your support system will help you stay steady, and your commitment to yourself will help you stay free.

Chapter 7: Picking Up the Pieces After the Game Ends

That first day after you've made the break - walking away from a business partnership, moving out of a shared home, or finally setting that firm boundary with a family member - feels like waking up on another planet. The air feels different. Everything looks strange. You're both lighter and heavier at the same time.

Managing Initial Chaos

THE CHAOS ISN'T ALWAYS what you expect. Sometimes, it's loud - phones ringing, angry messages, flying monkeys swooping in. But sometimes, and this can be even more unsettling, it's completely quiet. That silence can be deafening.

Let me tell you about Natalie's first week after leaving her covert narcissist business partner. She'd prepared for World War III. Instead, she got... nothing. Complete radio silence. "The silence was worse than any fight," she said. "I kept waiting for something to happen. Every email notification made my heart race. Every phone call could be the one. The anticipation was exhausting."

This is where many people stumble - in that space between expecting chaos and getting silence or preparing for silence and getting chaos. The covert narcissist knows this. They've studied you long enough to know which would destabilize you more.

Then there's the internal chaos - the constant second-guessing, the waves of relief followed by tsunamis of doubt, the moments of fierce certainty crashed by periods of devastating uncertainty. This is normal. Your internal compass is recalibrating after years of being redirected.

Natalie kept waiting for some kind of closure—a fight, a discussion, even an angry email. Instead, her business partner just vanished. There was no response to emails about final accounts, no acknowledgment of shared clients, no closure on projects they'd built together, just a void where answers should be.

This, too, is a form of control. Her partner maintained power over Natalie's emotional state by refusing to engage and leaving everything hanging. Every unfinished conversation, every unanswered question became a hook still embedded in Natalie's mind. She ran imaginary conversations, planning responses to confrontations that never came, stuck in an emotional limbo.

Let's contrast this with Amy's experience when she left her partner, Greg. Unlike Natalie, Greg launched an entire hoovering campaign: "I've changed. I'm in therapy now." "No one will ever understand you like I do." "Remember how magical it was in the beginning? We can have that again."

Hoovering - named after the vacuum cleaner - is when they try to suck you back in. They study your vulnerabilities and use them as entry points:

- If you're compassionate, they'll be in crisis
- If you're responsible, they'll need your help
- If you're spiritual, they'll have an awakening
- If you're practical, they'll have a logical proposal

The hardest part? Sometimes, they seem to mean it. They might even believe it themselves in the moment. But here's the truth: Whether they respond with silence like Natalie's partner or hoovering like Greg, it's all about control. One withdraws it, the other overwhelms with it, but both are trying to maintain their power over your emotional state.

Picture Lydia's world the month after she left her covert narcissist friend Caroline. They'd been part of what seemed like a magical circle of friends for five years. These women had shared everything on weekend brunches, group texts, and holiday celebrations. Or so Lydia thought.

Within weeks of setting boundaries with Caroline, Lydia watched her entire social world dissolve. The group chat went quiet. Her invitations to coffee were met with vague excuses. Photos of gatherings she wasn't invited to appeared on social media. The silence from her "friends" was deafening.

"I didn't just lose Caroline," Lydia explained. "I lost my entire community. People I'd celebrated birthdays with, shoulders I'd cried on, friends who'd been in my home... gone. And the worst part? I couldn't even be angry because most of them had no idea they were being manipulated."

That's the thing about flying monkeys - the term refers to people who, often unknowingly, do the covert narcissist's bidding. They're acting on a carefully crafted narrative that Caroline had been building for months or years: "Lydia's been so negative lately..." "She's going through something..." "I'm really worried about her..."

Now, contrast this with Trevor's experience leaving his business partner. His flying monkeys were more direct—mutual colleagues suddenly questioning his professional decisions, clients being told "concerning" stories about his stability, and vendors being warned about his "reliability." His former partner had spent years building professional relationships that could be weaponized.

"It was like dominoes falling," Trevor explained. "People I'd worked with for years started looking at me differently. Contracts mysteriously fell through. Suddenly, everyone was 'concerned' about my judgment."

Then there's Donna's family situation - her covert narcissist mother had spent decades building a network of relatives who would unknowingly do her bidding. Aunts, cousins, and even Donna's siblings became unwitting messengers: "Your mother just wants what's best for you..." "She's heartbroken by your distance..." "The family just isn't the same without you there..." "How can you do this to her after all she's sacrificed?"

The flying monkeys in family situations can be especially painful because they're people you've known your whole life, people you love, people you want to maintain relationships with. But they've been so thoroughly convinced of the covert narcissist's version of reality that having independent relationships with them becomes almost impossible.

Strategies for Handling Flying Monkeys and Social Fallout

STAY SILENT OR SPEAK Up?

Sometimes, the hardest decision is whether to defend yourself or keep silent. Here's what experience teaches us: Those who are meant to understand will seek to understand. Those who've already chosen sides won't be convinced by your explanations.

Setting Boundaries with Flying Monkeys: "I appreciate your concern, but this is between us." "I understand you care, but I'm not discussing this situation." "You have your perspective, and I respect that. I have mine."

The Web of Shared Connections

ONE OF THE MOST PAINFUL parts of breaking free from a covert narcissist is realizing how deeply they've woven themselves into your social fabric. It's not just about losing one relationship - it's about evaluating an entire network of connections that suddenly feel uncertain.

Let me tell you about BJ's awakening. BJ, a successful entrepreneur, found herself in a toxic friendship with a covert narcissist. After breaking free, she realized that the shared friendships she had maintained with the same enthusiasm were not as they seemed. The responses were different; the energy had shifted, and she asked herself uncomfortable questions: Why was she always the one trying? Why did she feel like her actions were being reported back to her former friend?

The most brutal realization wasn't just that some friends might be acting as unwitting 'flying monkeys'-as discussed before is a term used to describe people who unknowingly or knowingly enable a narcissist's behavior - it was understanding that these patterns of always being the connector, the teacher, and the maintainer of relationships might have been part of what made her vulnerable to covert narcissistic abuse in the first place.

BJ made a radical choice. She decided to wipe her social slate clean, like erasing a chalkboard. She adjusted her social media settings so certain people couldn't see her posts. She stopped being the one to always reach out. She became more guarded about sharing details of her new business ventures. With some connections, she maintained professional courtesy-being polite and respectful in her interactions-but created emotional distance-not sharing personal details or engaging in deep conversations. With others, she implemented a complete block.

"It felt paranoid at first," she admitted. "But I realized I needed to take my power back in every possible way, including the power to choose who gets access to my life and on what terms."

This isn't about becoming permanently closed off or distrustful. It's about creating space to discover who remains in your life when you're no longer doing all the maintenance. It's about learning who reaches out because they genuinely care about you, not because they're gathering information or maintaining social obligations.

Sometimes, healing means temporarily stepping back from an entire social network, even if some of those people are innocent bystanders. Until you can clearly see who's who, creating distance is not paranoia—it's protection. And with this protection comes a sense of clarity and peace, knowing that you're safeguarding your well-being.

Social Reorganization

NAVIGATING THIS SOCIAL restructuring is a powerful act of courage and wisdom. It's not about burning bridges or becoming permanently isolated—it's about taking control and consciously choosing who gets to be part of your rebuilt life and on what terms.

Think about concentric circles of trust. Some people might need to be moved from your inner circle to your outer circle, others might need to stay in a strictly professional zone, and some relationships might need to end entirely. This isn't about punishment; it's about protection and energy preservation.

BJ discovered something interesting as she stepped back. Some people she thought were close friends never reached out once she stopped initiating. Others, who she'd considered more peripheral, suddenly showed up with genuine concern and support. The landscape of her relationships shifted, but it became something more authentic, truer to who she was.

She also learned to trust her instincts about information sharing. When she felt that flutter of anxiety about sharing specific details of her life with someone, she honored it. Not every connection needs to know everything, and not every question deserves a complete answer. She developed what she called her "need to know" policy—sharing only what felt completely safe and comfortable.

Most importantly, she learned that true friends understand boundaries. They respect your need for space without demanding explanations. They don't take sides or relay information. They maintain their direct relationship with you, independent of other connections, giving you the freedom to be yourself.

This reorganization period can feel lonely at times. You might find yourself with a smaller social circle initially. But what you lose in quantity, you gain in quality. You create space for new connections that aren't tangled in old patterns. You develop relationships based on mutual effort and respect rather than obligation or habit.

The Questions and Pressure

ONE OF THE TRICKIEST parts of this social reorganization is handling the inevitable questions. Well-meaning friends might say things like: "But she asks about you all the time..." "Can't we all just get together like before?" "Why can't you two work it out?"

BJ developed her 'peaceful clause' - a simple, drama-free response that didn't invite debate. It was a powerful tool, allowing her to assert her boundaries with confidence: 'I've decided to make some changes in my life, and I appreciate you respecting that.' No explanations, no accusations, no defending her position.

Sometimes, the pressure comes in subtler forms: the casual mention of your name in their conversations with the narcissist, the 'accidental' sharing of your information, and the well-intentioned but boundary-crossing attempts to 'fix' things. This is where your new boundaries, such as limiting information shared with others or refusing unsolicited advice, get tested.

BJ was invited to events where she knew her former friend would be present. Instead of making excuses or creating drama, she declined when she felt uncomfortable attending. She didn't explain why, and she didn't ask who else would be there. She just honored her own comfort level, feeling reassured and confident in her decision.

The most powerful lesson? You don't owe anyone an explanation for protecting your peace. True friends will respect your boundaries without needing to understand all the details. Those who push, pry, or pressure you to explain why they might need to be part of your social distancing plan.

Over time, this new way of engaging creates a natural sorting process. People adjust to your new boundaries, or they don't. They respect your privacy, or they don't. They maintain a direct relationship with you, or they don't. This process helps you identify who respects your boundaries and who doesn't, guiding you in restructuring your social world.

Building New Connections

STARTING OVER IN A social or family setting can feel overwhelming. After being entangled in a web of complicated relationships, even the thought of putting yourself out there again might feel exhausting. But here's the beautiful part—you get to start fresh, armed with wisdom you didn't have before, and this new beginning is a source of empowerment and optimism.

BJ started small. She joined a business networking group with no previous connections. There was no shared history, no complicated dynamics, just fresh ground to plant new relationships. She found herself naturally more observant and more patient in developing connections. She wasn't jumping into instant intimacy or "soul friend" connections.

The key is finding communities based on genuine shared interests rather than shared people. It could be a book club, a spiritual group, a professional organization, or a hobby class. The focus stays on the shared activity rather than intense personal connections, allowing relationships to develop naturally and comfortably.

Most importantly, you bring your new wisdom with you. You recognize the red flags you might have missed before. You understand that healthy relationships develop gradually. Real connections don't require you to constantly prove your loyalty or worth, and this understanding fosters patience and a deeper understanding of others.

Remember: Thoughtfully rebuilding your social world isn't isolation - it's protection. And those who are meant to be part of your new chapter will respect the pace at which you write it, providing you with a sense of security and reassurance.

Managing the Social Media Minefield

SOCIAL MEDIA CAN BECOME a battlefield after a split with a covert narcissist. Your options:

- Temporary deactivation while the dust settles
- Careful curation of what you can see and who can see you

- Focus on building new connections rather than monitoring old ones

Handling Group Dynamics

IN PROFESSIONAL SETTINGS, stick to facts and documentation. Keep communications brief, professional, and in writing. Remember: Your work speaks for itself.

In social circles, accept that some friends are situational. Focus on the few who seek to understand rather than the many who take the narcissist's narrative.

In family situations, create individual relationships where possible. Some family members may come around after seeing patterns over time.

Emergency Self-Protection

WHEN FLYING MONKEYS become aggressive:

- Document everything
- Keep all communication in writing
- Set clear, firm boundaries
- Be prepared to distance yourself temporarily or permanently
- Seek legal counsel if harassment occurs

The Emergency Self-Care Survival Guide

WHEN YOUR WORLD FEELS like it's crumbling, self-care isn't optional - it's essential. But let's be real: this isn't about bubble baths and scented candles. This is about emotional and mental survival.

First, the Basics Matter More Than Ever

YOUR NERVOUS SYSTEM is probably in overdrive right now. You might swing between anxiety and numbness, between hypervigilance and exhaustion. Start with the fundamentals:

Sleep when you can, even if it means taking a sick day or just taking a nap. Your brain needs rest to process what's happening.

Eat something. Your body needs fuel, even if your stomach is in knots. Eat simple foods, small portions, or whatever stays down.

Move your body gently. Walk around the block, do some stretches, or do anything to keep the anxiety from getting stuck in your muscles.

Protecting Your Mental Space

TURN OFF NOTIFICATIONS if you need to. The world won't end if you don't respond immediately to texts or emails. Give yourself permission to be unavailable.

Find one safe person who gets it—just one. Someone who won't tell you what to do or how to feel, someone who can just sit with you in the mess.

Create small pockets of peace - even if it's just five minutes of breathing in your car before work. These moments add up.

The Practical Stuff

KEEP A BOTTLE OF WATER with you. Stress dehydrates you. Have simple snacks available. Keep your important documents somewhere safe. Have a go-bag packed if you need it. Keep some cash on hand for emergencies.

Most importantly, remember that however you're feeling right now is okay. If you're angry, be angry. If you're sad, be sad. If you're relieved and guilty about feeling relieved, that's okay, too. You're not crazy for having feelings about a crazy situation.

First Steps to Stability: Finding Your Footing

THEY SAY THE JOURNEY of a thousand miles begins with a single step. But they don't tell you that sometimes that first step feels impossible when your world has been turned upside down. Let's talk about how to find solid ground again.

Creating a New Normal

START WITH ONE SMALL routine. Just one. It could be morning coffee in silence. It could be an evening walk. Something that's just yours that no one can take away or mess with. This becomes your anchor point.

Stability is built in small moments, not grand gestures. It's about creating tiny islands of predictability in a chaotic ocean.

Practical Stability Steps

MAKE YOUR SPACE FEEL safe—even if it's just one room, one corner. Clean sheets, fresh air, a plant—something that says, "This is mine, and it's okay here."

Set one boundary and keep it. You may decide not to answer phone calls after 8 PM. You could block flying monkeys on social media. Pick something manageable and stick to it.

Financial stability matters, too. Start separating any entangled finances. Open a new bank account if you need to. Get clarity on your money situation, even if it's scary.

The Emotional Foundation

HERE'S SOMETHING CRUCIAL: Stability isn't about constantly feeling good. It's about knowing you can handle feeling bad. It's about building trust with yourself again.

Start making promises to yourself—small ones at first: "I will take a shower today." "I will eat lunch." "I will go to bed by 11." Each promise is a brick in the foundation of your new life.

Remember: Stability after leaving a covert narcissist isn't about getting back to normal - it's about creating a new normal. One that's actually healthy this time.

The most challenging truth about finding stability after leaving a covert narcissist is this: Some days will still feel wobbly. You'll have moments where you question everything. That's not a sign of failure - it's part of the process.

Think of stability as something like learning to walk again. At first, every step feels uncertain. You might stumble. You might need support. But gradually, step by step, you find your balance. You learn to trust your feet again.

The most important thing to remember during this phase is that stability isn't about perfection. It's about progress. It's about creating a foundation solid enough to support the more profound healing that comes next.

Once you've managed the initial chaos, dealt with the hoovering or silence, handled the flying monkeys, and found your essential stability, there's still significant work to do. Now comes the real healing - understanding those trauma bonds that kept you there, breaking free from the addiction to the chaos, and learning to trust yourself again.

In our next chapter, we'll dive deep into the recovery process. We'll explore why breaking free from a covert narcissist feels like withdrawing from a drug, why your body might crave the very person who hurt you, and how to rebuild yourself from the ground up.

Chapter 8: Resetting the Pieces – The Path to Healing

Understanding how trauma bonds form in these seemingly divine connections is perhaps the most crucial part of healing. Let me tell you something that might help you feel less crazy: Even those of us who've studied personality disorders for years can miss the signs of a covert narcissist. Why? Because they often appear as the answer to our prayers - the perfect friend, partner, or colleague who 'gets' us on a soul level. But beware, their seemingly divine nature is a carefully crafted facade, a deception that can be hard to see through.

Think about it: We're all human. We all have seasons of struggle, moments of self-centeredness, and times when we're not our best selves. That's normal. What makes covert narcissism different is the intention—or rather, the lack of intention—to truly look inward and grow.

Let me share something personal: Writing this book has shown me my own blind spots and character defects that need attention. That's healthy—that ability to look at ourselves with both honesty and compassion. But here's where it differs from what we see in covert narcissists: They use therapy, spirituality, and self-help language as weapons rather than tools for genuine growth.

Consider Angela's experience with her "soul friend" Janice. They met at a church retreat, and it seemed divinely orchestrated. Janice spoke the language of personal growth perfectly: "We're here to help each other heal..." "Our souls chose this friendship..." "God brought us together for a reason..."

Even as Angela's counselor, I was initially impressed by Janice's apparent insight and support. Because here's the tricky part - covert narcissists often use the language of healing to avoid actually healing.

When Angela met Janice at that spiritual retreat, it felt like finding her soul's missing piece. Janice seemed to embody everything Angela aspired to be - spiritually evolved, emotionally aware, and deeply compassionate. Their connection felt almost mystical.

"It was like she could see right into my soul," Angela told me. "She knew exactly what to say, exactly how to support me. She used all the right spiritual language, quoted all the right teachers, and seemed so committed to growth."

The trauma bond formed subtly, wrapped in the language of spiritual connection: "We're meant to trigger each other for healing..." "This discomfort you're feeling is just your ego resisting growth..." "Your reaction to me shows where you still need to do work..."

See how masterful that is? Every boundary Angela tried to set became evidence of her "spiritual work still to do." Every hurt she expressed became her "attachment to the world." Every concern she raised became her "resistance to divine timing."

This is why trauma bonds with covert narcissists who use spiritual language are so powerful - they hijack our deepest yearning for meaning and connection. They make us question not just our judgment but our very spiritual journey.

I remember sitting with Angela in a session months later, watching her struggle with the aftermath: "How could something that felt so divinely guided be so toxic? Was I wrong about everything I felt? Can I ever trust my spiritual intuition again?"

Learning to trust your inner knowing again is the hardest part of healing from spiritual manipulation. Because here's the truth: True spiritual connections don't demand you abandon yourself. Real soul connections make you feel more like yourself, not less. Trust in yourself is the key to breaking free from the chains of manipulation and reclaiming your true self.

But covert narcissists are experts at blurring these lines. They use universal truths to mask personal manipulation: 'Everything happens for a reason...' (so don't question their behavior) 'We're all one...' (so your boundaries are 'separation') 'Trust God or the universe...' (translation: trust their control). This is not just manipulation, it's a form of spiritual warfare, a battle for your mind and soul that you may not even realize you're in.

But this manipulation isn't limited to spiritual realms. Let's look at how it plays out in other contexts:

In business partnerships, they use the language of entrepreneurship: "Visionaries think differently..." "Real leaders take risks..." "Success requires sacrifice..."

In romantic relationships, they hijack the language of love: "No one will understand you like I do..." "Our connection is too special to be understood by others..." "Real love means accepting all parts of me..."

In friendships, they use the language of loyalty: "True friends stick together no matter what..." "Family doesn't abandon family..." "After all we've been through..."

The common thread? They take universal truths or deeply held values and twist them into chains. They use our own beliefs, integrity, and commitments against us. And because the manipulation aligns with values we already hold dear, it's harder to spot and break free from.

The Push-Pull of Potential and Helplessness

THERE'S SOMETHING PARTICULARLY seductive about how covert narcissists present themselves - they're simultaneously superior and helpless, visionary and victimized. They're holding up a mirror to your potential while claiming they need your help to reach theirs.

"I have this amazing vision," they'll say, eyes sparkling with possibility. "And you're the only one who really gets it. You have exactly what I'm missing..."

They position themselves as both the teacher and the student, the guru and the seeker. One day, they share profound wisdom about life, business, or spirituality. The next day, they're helpless with technology, overwhelmed by basic tasks, or "too creative" to handle details.

This dance is masterful because it hooks your nurturing instincts and ambitions: "With your organizational skills and my vision..." "You're so good at the things I struggle with..." "Together, we could create something amazing..."

They paint pictures of grand futures while perpetually unable to handle the present. Their potential becomes a carrot they dangle—always visible but never quite reachable. And you, with your genuine desire to help and your ability to see the best in others, become invested in helping them reach this potential. You might even encourage them and boost their ego out of true support.

The trauma bond strengthens because it makes you feel both needed and special. You become the chosen one who understands their greatness, the faithful supporter who sees past their struggles, and the loyal friend who believes in their dreams.

Breaking Free While Keeping Your Heart Intact

THE HARDEST PART ABOUT breaking trauma bonds with a covert narcissist isn't just the separation - it's maintaining your capacity to care without being consumed. Because here's the truth: Your ability to see potential in others, your desire to help, and your willingness to support dreams aren't weaknesses. They're beautiful qualities that were exploited.

Think about how they hooked you: "No one understands my vision like you do..." "You're the missing piece I've been waiting for..." "With your help, I could finally..."

And you, genuinely wanting to help others succeed, got pulled into their orbit. You invested your time, energy, skills, and heart into their potential. You became emotionally invested in their success, growth, and dreams.

Breaking free means understanding that someone else's potential isn't your responsibility. Their dreams aren't your job to fulfill, and their helplessness isn't your crisis to solve.

This is where real healing begins - in learning to separate genuine collaboration from exploitation. Real partnerships involve mutual growth, shared effort, and reciprocal support, whether in business, friendship, or love. They don't need one person to constantly prop up the other's potential while depleting themselves.

The question isn't "How do I stop caring about others?" but "How do I care about others while staying whole myself?"

Caring with Boundaries: The Path Forward

THINK OF YOUR COMPASSION like a beautiful garden. Just because you have a garden doesn't mean everyone gets to pick your flowers. Some people can admire it from outside the fence. Some can sit with you among the blooms. But no one gets to uproot your entire garden in the name of helping them grow their own.

Start with small boundaries: "I can listen, but I can't take this on for you." "I believe in your potential, but you must do the work." "I care about your success, but not at the expense of my well-being."

Watch their response to these gentle boundaries. A healthy person will respect them. A covert narcissist will try to make you feel guilty for having them: "I thought you believed in me..." "No one else understands like you do..." "I guess I was wrong about our special connection..."

Here's the crucial part: You can hold space for someone's dreams without becoming responsible for them. You can believe in someone's potential without sacrificing yourself to help them reach it. You can be compassionate without being consumed.

Remember this truth: Real support energizes both people. If you're constantly drained while they're constantly dreaming, that's not a partnership - that's a parasitic relationship dressed up as potential.

Finding Your Voice and Trusting It Again

ONE OF THE TRICKIEST parts of recovery is learning to trust your inner voice again—that quiet knowing that got muffled under all their grand visions and subtle manipulations. It's like tuning a radio back to its own frequency after years of static.

Start small. Notice what lights you up versus what drains you. Not what they said should excite you, not what looks good on paper, but what actually makes your soul hum. It could be smaller dreams than their grand visions. It could be quieter successes. That's okay.

Pay attention to your body's signals: That flutter in your stomach when something feels off, the tension in your shoulders when you're being manipulated, the exhaustion that comes after interactions, and the lightness you feel when you're truly aligned.

Your body knew the truth long before your mind caught up. Now it's time to listen.

Building back self-trust happens in tiny moments:

- When you honor a small boundary
- When you say no to something that doesn't feel right
- When you pursue your own dreams, however modest they might seem
- When you choose yourself without guilt

Most importantly, recognize that healing isn't about becoming invulnerable; It's about staying open while being wise. It's about maintaining your capacity for genuine connection while strengthening your ability to discern who deserves that connection.

Healthy Boundaries While Keeping Your Heart Open

THE ART OF BOUNDARIES isn't about building walls—it's about installing good gates. You decide what comes in and what stays out, and you choose when the gate opens and closes.

Think of it like hosting a dinner party. Just because you're a fantastic host doesn't mean:

- Everyone gets invited
- Guests can stay indefinitely
- People can raid your kitchen without asking
- Visitors get to redecorate your home

Your generosity isn't a blank check; others can cash whenever they want. Your gifts aren't community property, and your energy isn't a public utility.

Here's what healthy giving looks like: "I can help with this specific task." "I'm available during these hours." "I can offer this much support." "Here's what I'm able to contribute."

Notice how different this feels from the endless, boundary-less giving that covert narcissists demand. You're still helping, contributing, and being your compassionate self - but with clarity and limits.

Remember: The right people will respect your boundaries. The wrong people will call them selfish. And that reaction tells you everything you need to know about who deserves your energy.

The Boundary Paradox

HERE'S SOMETHING THAT often confuses people about covert narcissists: They either have no boundaries or rigid, harsh ones - and sometimes both at the same time. But when it comes to your boundaries? Those might as well be drawn in invisible ink.

Watch how they handle boundaries: "Oh, I must have misunderstood..." (as they glide right past your clearly stated limit) "I hear what you're saying, but..." (followed by why your boundary doesn't apply) "That's not really going to work for me..." (dismissing your needs entirely)

The most maddening part? They do this so smoothly that you sit silently, knowing that speaking up is pointless. They've already decided how things will go. Your boundaries aren't just crossed - they're irrelevant to their agenda.

This is actually one of the biggest red flags in any relationship - when you realize that expressing your needs or setting limits is utterly useless because they'll do what they want anyway. You find yourself going along to avoid the exhausting dance of them pretending to listen while completely disregarding your boundaries.

As we move into our next chapter about long-term healing, remember this: Someone who consistently ignores, dismisses, or glides past your boundaries isn't just disrespecting your limits - they're telling you exactly who they are. And sometimes, the healthiest boundary is the one that shows them the door.

Long-term healing will show us how to move forward and create relationships in which our boundaries aren't just heard—they're respected.

Breaking the Addiction

LET'S TALK ABOUT SOMETHING that feels shameful but shouldn't: the addiction to a covert narcissist. It's not just emotional - it's biochemical. Your brain literally gets hooked on the cycle of hope and disappointment, connection and abandonment, validation and devaluation.

Think about the pattern: They love-bomb you with attention and understanding, then withdraw, leaving you craving that connection. They return with just enough warmth to keep you hoping, and then they pull away again, and the cycle continues.

Your brain releases dopamine during the good times, cortisol during the stress, adrenaline with the anxiety, and oxytocin when they show moments of care. It's like being on an emotional roller coaster that your body chemistry starts to crave.

Breaking this addiction means going through actual withdrawal. You'll have moments where you desperately want to reach out, check their social media, and find some connection - any connection - to them. This isn't a weakness. This is your brain chemistry adjusting to a new normal.

The hardest truth? Sometimes, you'll miss them even while understanding how toxic they are. You'll miss:

- The intensity of the connection

- The magic of those good moments
- The dream of what could have been
- The version of them they first showed you

Handling the Withdrawal

JUST LIKE ANY ADDICTION, the first few weeks and months are the hardest. You'll have moments where the urge to contact them feels almost physical. Your body and brain will try to convince you: "Maybe it wasn't that bad..." "Things could be different this time..." "No one else understands me like they did..."

This is when you need to remember: What you're missing isn't really them - it's the biochemical high of those perfect moments. You're missing the person they pretended to be, not who they are.

Think of breaking this addiction like detoxing - it's going to feel uncomfortable before it feels better. You might experience:

- Intense longing for the good times
- Anxiety about being alone
- Depression as your brain chemistry rebalances
- Waves of doubt about your decision

This is where rebuilding self-trust begins. Each time you resist reaching out, you tell yourself, "I choose my well-being." Each time you sit with the discomfort, you rebuild trust in yourself instead of returning to it.

Collect evidence of your strength: Remember how you functioned before them. Notice how much calmer you feel without the chaos. Please pay attention to the energy you have now that you're not managing their emotions and recognize how your other relationships are improving.

The most powerful moment comes when you realize that the peace of being true to yourself feels better than the high of their validation ever did.

Finding Your Voice Again

THINK BACK TO WHO YOU were before them. Remember how you used to speak up, share ideas, and express needs? That person isn't gone – they were just quietly waiting backstage while someone else ran the show.

At first, your voice might come out shaky. You might second-guess every opinion and every feeling. That's normal. You've spent so long filtering your thoughts through their potential reactions that speaking your raw truth feels dangerous.

Start small: Notice what you actually think about things without their influence. Please pay attention to your genuine reactions before editing them. Allow yourself to have opinions that differ from theirs and trust your memories of events.

Here's something powerful I've watched happen with clients: They'll be talking about something simple—like what kind of food they enjoy—and suddenly stop, realizing they're still describing things the way their covert narcissist would approve of them. Then comes the beautiful moment of recognition: "Wait... I actually don't like that restaurant. I just said I did because they always insisted it was the best."

These small moments of truth-telling build on each other. Each time you honor your real thoughts and feelings, your voice gets stronger. Each time you trust your own experience without needing their validation, your confidence grows.

Remember Something Crucial

THEY WERE DRAWN TO you for a reason - your gifts, light, abilities, and genuine warmth. Covert narcissists don't target weak people; they're attracted to strong people with beautiful qualities they wish they had. Your empathy, talent, vision, and ability to genuinely connect with others weren't flaws that got you into trouble. These are your superpowers that someone tried to hijack.

As you heal, you'll rediscover these gifts, but now with wisdom as their protector. You'll remember: You can lead that project without someone taking the credit. You can share your ideas without them being stolen. You can shine without someone dimming your light. You can laugh without being the butt of subtle jokes, and most of all, you can dream big without needing their validation.

The flattery they used to hook you? That was just a pale imitation of your actual worth. You don't need someone else to tell you you're unique - you already are. You don't need someone else's grand visions - you have your own.

Genuine relationships - whether business, romantic, or friendship - don't require you to shrink. They don't need constant flattery to sustain them. They don't thrive on subtle put-downs disguised as jokes. They grow in the soil of mutual respect, genuine appreciation, and authentic connection.

You're not just healing—you're remembering who you were always meant to be. And this time, you get to be that person without apology, without dimming your light, and without managing someone else's insecurities.

The greatest gift of healing from a covert narcissist isn't just freedom from them—it's freedom to be fully yourself. All that energy you spent managing their emotions, walking on eggshells, and trying to prove your worth? It's yours now—to create, to grow, and to thrive.

This journey isn't just about recovering from trauma bonds or breaking addictive patterns. It's about reclaiming your birthright to exist exactly as you are, without needing to earn it through constant giving or prove it through endless doing.

The next chapter of your life - whether in business, love, or friendship - will be different because you're different. Not more demanding, not more guarded, but more wisely open. You'll recognize authentic connections because you've learned to trust your intuition. You'll appreciate genuine compliments because they don't come with hidden hooks. You'll enjoy real collaboration because it doesn't drain your soul.

Remember: You're not just healing from something bad. You're healing into something beautiful - your most whole, authentic version. And that self doesn't need to be perfect to be worthy. Doesn't need to be exceptional to be valuable. Doesn't need to be anything other than authentically you.

As we move on, we'll explore how this foundation of self-trust and authentic power becomes your compass for navigating all future relationships. Because the best protection from future covert narcissists isn't walls—it's wisdom.

Chapter 9: Playing the Long Game – Pathways to Lasting Healing

Processing trauma looks different when you're dealing with covert narcissistic abuse. It's not just about healing from apparent wounds - it's about understanding how your perception of reality, trust, and self-worth were altered.

Think about Haylee, who bravely spent twenty years doubting her memories because her mother would so sweetly say, "Oh honey, that's not how it happened at all..." Or Kyle, who realized he'd spent a decade dimming his natural enthusiasm because his "soul mate" partner had convinced him he was "too much." Their courage in facing these challenges is truly inspiring.

The tricky part about processing this kind of trauma is that it often looks pristine on the surface. No raised voices. No obvious abuse. Just years of subtle erosion that left deep caves in your confidence.

Here's where forgiveness versus acceptance becomes crucial. Everyone will tell you to forgive. But what they don't understand is that with covert narcissists, some forms of so-called forgiveness can become another form of self-abandonment if we're not careful. Sometimes, acceptance is more powerful—accepting that this really happened, it really was that bad, and yes, your feelings are valid.

Real forgiveness is meant to heal. Forgiveness is not synonymous with reconciliation. You can accept and even forgive another person without allowing yourself to be used and abused. Forgiveness is about releasing the emotional grip a person has on you. This releases you from resentment, bitterness, control, judgment, and shame. It also releases the other person to deal with their own life and possibly work on their character defects. You let go and let God... live and let live, as they say in some of the recovery circles.

And this brings us to generational patterns. Often, we attract covert narcissists because their behavior feels familiar. Maybe you had a parent who used silent treatment as control. Perhaps you grew up walking on eggshells around someone's "sensitivity." These patterns feel like home until we learn to build a new home in healthier territory.

The Gift and the Wound

WHEN WE DIG INTO OUR family of origin work, we often find both the source of our vulnerability to covert narcissists and the seeds of our greatest strengths. Let me share something personal about this journey.

As an only child in a loving but dysfunctional home, I became the family peacemaker. Conflict wasn't just uncomfortable—it felt dangerous. I learned to read rooms before entering them, sense emotional undercurrents, and smooth rough waters before they could become storms. Sound familiar?

These same skills that made us excellent targets for covert narcissists are also our superpowers. That ability to read people? It's a gift. That deep empathy? It's precious. That desire to maintain harmony? It comes from a beautiful place. We don't need to destroy these parts of ourselves - we need to protect them better. Our experiences have made us resilient and strong.

The patterns run deep because they started early. Maybe you learned that love means walking on eggshells. Perhaps you discovered that keeping peace meant keeping quiet. Maybe you figured out that being "good" meant being available whenever someone needed you.

This is why working with a therapist who understands family systems is crucial. Because untangling these patterns isn't just about recognizing them - it's about understanding:

- Why they served us once
- How they're hurting us now
- Which parts to keep
- What needs to change

The goal isn't to stop being empathic or to become rigid. The goal is to be wisely compassionate, to maintain our sensitivity while building stronger boundaries, and to understand that our ability to sense others' needs shouldn't come at the cost of abandoning our own.

Family patterns and childhood adaptations run deep - they're written into our very cells. Many of us grew up learning to be hyper-aware of others' needs, developing an almost magical ability to sense emotional weather changes before they happened. These survival skills shaped us for better and worse.

Here's where the real magic of healing happens: We can go back and repair those early wounds. Whether you view it as psychological work or spiritual healing, connecting with and re-parenting your inner child creates profound change at a cellular level.

Imagine sitting with your young self - that sensitive child who learned to be the peacemaker and felt everything so deeply. What would you tell them? How would you protect them? What boundaries would you teach them to set?

This isn't just visualization - it's deep reprogramming. When we go back and imagine: "You don't have to fix everything." "Your feelings matter, too." "It's safe to speak up." "You can let others handle their own emotions."

Something shifts in our present-day responses. The hypervigilance starts to soften. The compulsive need to keep everyone happy begins to ease. We start parenting ourselves with the wisdom we've gained through our experiences.

This healing ripples forward and backward through time, changing how we react now and helping heal those original wounds. Our adult self becomes the protector our child self needed. The effectiveness of this healing process gives us hope for a brighter future.

Creating a Safe Space for Your Young Self

IMAGINE HAVING TEA with your younger self. What would your younger self tell you about what they needed back then? Maybe they needed someone to say, "Your sensitivity is a gift, not a problem." Perhaps they needed to hear, "You don't have to be perfect to be loved."

You can actually create this healing dialogue. Find a quiet space, maybe with a childhood photo or a beloved old toy and sit with that younger version of you. Listen to what they feared. Understand what made them feel safe. Show them the strength and wisdom you've gained.

Some people write letters: "Dear Little One, I see how hard you tried to keep everyone happy..." "I wish I could have told you then what I know now..." "You were so brave, feeling everything so deeply..."

Others have healing conversations in their mind: "You know what? It wasn't your job to fix the grown-ups." "Let me show you how to set boundaries while staying kind. "I'll protect you now. You can rest."

This isn't just fantasy work - it's rewiring your nervous system's earliest programming. When you comfort that inner child, you're changing how your adult self responds to similar situations.

The most beautiful part? You'll naturally set better boundaries in current relationships as you heal your inner child. You'll catch yourself starting to people-please and hear that wise inner parent say, "We don't need to earn love anymore. We're enough just as we are."

Processing trauma goes deeper than just talking about what happened. While our minds need to understand our experience, our bodies hold the deeper story. That constant tension in your shoulders, how your breath catches when someone raises their voice, how your stomach knots when you need to set a boundary - these are your body's memories speaking.

This is why healing often requires more than traditional therapy. Many survivors find profound relief in somatic experiencing, where they learn to listen to their bodies' stories. Others discover peace through EMDR, watching those stuck memories finally lose their emotional charge. Movement therapies, like yoga or dance, help release what words can't reach.

Once we can see them clearly, breaking generational patterns becomes possible. Maybe you notice how your grandmother's habit of "keeping the peace" at any cost lives in your own tendency to silence yourself. Or how your father's need to please everyone shaped your own relationship with boundaries. Seeing these patterns lets us choose different responses.

True resilience isn't about becoming invulnerable but staying soft while learning to protect that softness better. It's maintaining your ability to connect while developing a keener sense of who deserves that connection.

Finding meaning in our experiences sometimes reveals patterns that seem almost cosmically orchestrated. Consider this remarkable story: A young woman lands her dream job, only to discover that her HR manager is someone from her mother's past - a woman who, twenty-five years earlier, had ghosted her mother for choosing to stay with her boyfriend. Like a karmic echo, this old wound resurfaces in the next generation.

The HR manager, still carrying whatever drove her to ghost her friend decades ago, found a way to exercise that same control pattern again - this time by targeting the daughter with false accusations until she could engineer a reason to fire her. Some people don't change; they find new stages for old dramas.

But here's where meaning-making becomes powerful: Both mother and daughter had to face this experience not just as a random act of cruelty but as an opportunity for growth. They had to rise above the toxicity, like that Incubus song says, "Pardon me while I burn and rise above the flames." Sometimes, we need to burn the toxicity and rise above the situation. Sometimes, the universe hands us these seemingly unfair situations not to punish us but to teach us something essential about our own strength.

Finding meaning doesn't make what happened okay. It doesn't justify the HR manager's actions or erase the pain of losing a job unfairly. But it gives us a choice: We can stay caught in the story of unfairness, or we can use it as fuel for our evolution.

The lesson might be about recognizing patterns across generations, learning to trust our instincts earlier, and understanding that toxic people don't change unless they do the deep work—and that their unhealed wounds can still affect us decades later.

Sometimes, our most harrowing experiences become our greatest teachers. That unfair firing didn't just show how narcissistic patterns can echo through decades - it revealed something powerful about resilience, about how we can choose to rise above someone else's unhealed wounds.

Look at how many successful people have stories about being fired, undermined, or pushed out of situations by toxic people. They often say the same thing: "It was the best thing that could have happened to me, though I couldn't see it at the time." Not because the experience wasn't painful but because it forced them to grow beyond what they thought possible.

Finding meaning doesn't happen overnight. It comes in waves of understanding. You may first realize how the experience made you stronger. Then, you notice how it taught you to trust your instincts. Later, you see how it freed you from a situation that was limiting your growth. Finally, you understand how it prepared you for something better.

Think about how many empaths and healers come from challenging backgrounds. Their experiences didn't just hurt them - they shaped them into more compassionate, insightful people. The key is learning to use your experiences as stepping stones rather than letting them become anchors that hold you down.

This doesn't mean we should be grateful for abuse or manipulation. But it does mean we get to choose what we do with these experiences. Do we let them define us? Or do we let them refine us?

Our Healing Journey Becomes a Light for Others

WHEN WE FIND MEANING in our survival, something magical happens. Our story stops being just about pain and becomes about transformation. You may recognize the subtle signs of covert narcissism in a friend's relationship and can gently help them see what you couldn't see before. Your experience enables you to mentor younger colleagues and support healthy boundaries in professional relationships.

Your hard-earned wisdom becomes a gift you can share without preaching. It shows up in the way you model healthy boundaries, in how you can name manipulation tactics without bitterness, and in how you show that it's possible to stay compassionate while being wisely cautious.

I think about a client who went through a devastating experience with a covert narcissist at work. Years later, she found herself in a position to create workplace policies that protected others from similar situations. Her pain became purpose. Her experience became expertise. Her survival became a strength for others.

This kind of healing creates ripples. When you learn to trust your intuition again, you help others trust theirs. When you demonstrate that it's possible to recover from betrayal without becoming bitter, you show others a path forward. When you share your story with someone who's where you once were, you become the guide you wished you'd had.

But remember: You don't owe your story to anyone. Share it only when and if it feels right. Sometimes, the meaning we find in survival is deeply personal, and that's okay, too.

A Deeper Truth About Long-Term Healing

THE JOURNEY OF HEALING from covert narcissistic abuse isn't linear, and it doesn't have a neat endpoint where we can say, "Now I'm completely healed." Instead, it's more like tending a garden - there's always more growing to do, more beauty to uncover, more wisdom to gain.

Some days, you'll feel strong and certain, sharing your story with others who need to hear it. Other days, an old trigger might catch you off guard, reminding you that healing has layers. Both experiences are valid and part of the journey.

What matters isn't that we never struggle again - it's that we know how to find our way back to center when we do. We learn to trust ourselves even when we're shaken. We discover that our sensitivity, adequately protected, is still our greatest gift.

Remember this: You didn't just survive; you learned. You didn't just heal; you transformed. Your experience, though painful, has given you a kind of emotional sight that others might not have. You can spot the subtle signs, feel the shift in energy, and sense when something's off. These aren't paranoid reactions—they're hard-earned wisdom.

As we move into our next chapter about rebuilding your life, know that your healing journey isn't just about returning to who you were before. It's about becoming who you were always meant to be—stronger, wiser, and more authentically yourself than ever before.

Chapter 10: A New Game: Writing Your Rules for Life

Remember who you were before them? That person who had dreams, opinions, favorite foods, and quirky habits? They're still there, waiting to emerge again. Rebuilding your life isn't just about healing from trauma - it's about rediscovering yourself piece by precious piece.

Reclaiming Your Identity

THINK ABOUT AUTUMN, who realized six months after leaving her covert narcissist business partner that she actually hated green smoothies. "I'd been drinking them every morning because she insisted they were essential for 'high vibe' entrepreneurs," Autumn told me, laughing. "Turns out I'm more of a bacon and eggs person. Always was."

These small reclamations matter. You may start listening to music they criticized. Maybe you wear clothes they subtly disapproved of. You may laugh loudly again, take up space, and voice opinions.

The rebuilding starts with simple questions: What do I actually like? What did I used to dream about? What makes me smile? What feels like me?

Sometimes, you'll discover that you've changed - that some of their influences resonated with your authentic self. That's okay, too. The key is choosing consciously now, not living by their prescriptions.

The most beautiful part of reclaiming your identity is realizing you get to keep evolving. You're not going backwards to who you were before them. You're moving forward into who you're becoming, taking only what truly serves your growth.

Creating New Patterns

AFTER YEARS OF WALKING on eggshells or managing someone else's reality, creating healthy patterns feels almost foreign. It's like learning to walk again - wobbly at first, but gradually finding your balance.

Let me tell you about Marcus, who spent five years running his business around his partner's chaos. Every morning started with checking his phone for crisis messages. Every decision required hours of emotional management. After the split, he found himself almost afraid of the quiet.

"I didn't know what to do with peace," he admitted. "I kept waiting for the other shoe to drop. It took months to realize I could just... work. Make decisions. Move forward without managing anyone else's emotions."

Creating new patterns starts with minor changes. You could begin your day with quiet instead of checking messages. You could make one decision without seeking anyone's approval. Maybe you let yourself rest without feeling guilty.

The trick is building routines that support your growth rather than someone else's needs. Setting aside time for creativity that's just for you, making decisions based on what you want, not what others expect, creating space for rest without having to earn it, and trusting your judgment about what needs to be done.

What's fascinating is how these new patterns ripple into every area of your life. When you start honoring your rhythms, you naturally attract people and opportunities that respect them, too.

Building Healthy Relationships

AFTER A COVERT NARCISSIST, healthy relationships can feel almost dull at first. Where's the drama? The intensity? The magical "understanding" they claimed to have of your soul? But here's what you start to notice: Real connection feels like peace, not fireworks.

Think about those first few friendships or professional relationships after getting free. You might find yourself waiting for the other shoe to drop. Expecting the subtle dig wrapped in a compliment. Bracing for the moment, they'll use your vulnerability against you.

But gradually, something beautiful happens. You discover that healthy people:

- Mean what they say
- Respect your boundaries without making you feel guilty
- Allow you to have different opinions
- Don't need you to dim your light so they can shine

The real gift comes when you realize you're no longer exhausted after interactions. You're not mentally reviewing conversations for hidden meanings. You're not managing someone else's emotions while ignoring your own.

Healthy relationships allow both people to exist fully. There's space for differences, growth, and genuine give and take. Most importantly, there's room for you to be authentically yourself—quirks, boundaries, needs, and all.

Remember: You're not just learning to trust others again. You're learning to trust yourself to choose better relationships. Your radar for manipulation is actually sharper now, not paranoid. Remember those gut feelings you learned to ignore? They're your built-in wisdom speaking.

Career and Financial Recovery

WHETHER A COVERT NARCISSIST impacted your business partnerships, derailed your career path, or drained your finances, rebuilding your professional and financial life takes courage. But here's the surprising part - without someone constantly undermining your confidence or creating chaos, you might thrive in ways you never expected.

Look at Misty, who left her successful coaching practice because her business partner had created such a toxic environment. Starting over felt terrifying. "I thought I'd lose all my clients," she told me. "But what actually happened was that without her constant drama and need to control everything, I had the energy to create something even better."

Financial recovery often starts with reclaiming your sense of capability. Maybe they convinced you that you couldn't handle money without them. Perhaps they created such constant emergencies that saving felt impossible. Maybe they subtly undermined every financial decision you made. Maybe you were so overwhelmed that you made some bad decisions because you were doing too much.

The rebuilding process isn't just about money—it's about reclaiming your power. It might mean Taking control of your accounts, making financial decisions without second-guessing yourself, building emergency savings so you never feel trapped again, and trusting your professional judgment.

Sometimes, recovery looks like taking a step back to move forward, like Mario, who initially chose to take a lower-paying job after leaving his toxic partnership. "For the first time in years, I could just do my work without managing someone else's emotions," he said. That peace was worth more than money."

And here's the thing about career recovery - once you're not spending all your energy managing someone else's needs or drama, you might be surprised by how much you can accomplish.

Finding Joy Again... And Beyond

THERE'S THIS MOMENT in recovery when you catch yourself laughing - really laughing - and realize you can't remember the last time you felt this light. Joy creeps back in slowly, like a sunrise after a long night.

At first, it almost feels wrong to be happy. You're waiting for someone to comment on your joy being "too much" or remind you of all the serious things you should focus on instead. But gradually, you remember that you can feel good without earning it.

This natural joy becomes the bridge to truly thriving beyond mere survival. Because thriving isn't about achieving some perfect state—it's about creating a new normal where you can be fully yourself.

As we move into our closing chapter about thriving beyond survival, remember this: You're not just recovering from something terrible. You're growing into something beautiful—a life where joy isn't something you have to justify, strength isn't something you have to prove, and authenticity isn't something you have to fight for.

Thriving beyond survival will show us how to take all these rebuilt pieces - your reclaimed identity, your new patterns, your healthy relationships, your professional recovery, and your rediscovered joy - and weave them into a life that's not just free from covert narcissistic influence, but rich with authentic purpose.

Chapter 11: A New Game Begins: Your Rules, Your Power

There's a quote that says, "Life begins at the end of your comfort zone." But for those who've survived covert narcissistic abuse, I'd change that to say: "Life begins when you finally get comfortable being yourself again."

Creating your new normal isn't about becoming a different person. It's about rediscovering and accepting your authentic self, now equipped with the wisdom that only experience can bring. It's about recognizing that you can be wise, open-hearted, cautious, generous, strong, and soft.

Think about those moments when you realize you're no longer just surviving but thriving. It may be when you share your story and hear your own strength in your voice. It may be when you help someone else spot the red flags you once missed. It could be simply waking up and feeling peaceful in your own space and skin.

Your new normal might look quieter than your old life, but it's not devoid of excitement. It might not have the dramatic highs and lows, the intensity that once felt like passion. Instead, it has something better: authenticity, real connections, and genuine peace.

Do you want to know the most beautiful part? Recognizing that everything you went through has given you a kind of emotional wisdom that can't be learned from books. You've earned your PhD in human nature the hard way. Now, you get to use that wisdom to protect yourself and help light the way for others, feeling confident and capable in your journey.

This hard-earned wisdom becomes both your protection and your gift to others. You learn to recognize authenticity because you've experienced its opposite. You understand the value of boundaries because you know the cost of not having them. You appreciate genuine connections because you've known hollow ones.

The strength you find isn't the hard, defensive kind. It's the quiet confidence of knowing yourself and being comfortable with that truth. It's the ability to say "no" without explanation when something feels off. It's the wisdom to trust your intuition while keeping your heart open.

Helping others comes naturally, but differently now. You don't need to save anyone - you share what you know when asked. Your story becomes a lantern for others finding their way through similar darkness. But this time, you know how to help without depleting yourself.

I think about one of my clients, Carmen, who now mentors young entrepreneurs. "I can spot the signs of manipulation in business partnerships now," she says. "When someone shares their struggles, I don't just empathize - I can actually help them set healthy boundaries from the start."

Living authentically becomes your new superpower. You no longer need to shape-shift to please others or dim your light to make anyone comfortable. You get to be gloriously, imperfectly you—with all your quirks, passions, ideas, and boundaries.

When you start living authentically, something remarkable happens in your relationships. Like ripples in a pond, your truth-telling creates waves of authenticity around you. Real recognizes real, as they say.

You naturally attract people who appreciate boundaries because you model them so clearly. Your professional relationships are clearer because you're no longer afraid to state your needs. Your friendships have more depth because they're built on genuine connection rather than constant giving.

I remember watching this unfold with Eric after he rebuilt his business. "The strangest thing," he told me, "Is that I'm actually making more money while working less. It turns out that when you're not constantly managing someone else's chaos, you have the energy to grow."

Or consider Camille, who worried she'd never trust enough to love again. She discovered that healthy love feels completely different. "It's calm," she says. "We can disagree without drama. I can have bad days without worrying he'll use them against me. I can be myself without editing."

This is what thriving looks like - not a perfect life, but an authentic one. You'll still have challenges, but you'll face them as yourself, not as someone's supporting character. You'll still have doubts, but they'll be honest questions, not manipulated confusion. This transformation from surviving to thriving should fill you with hope and optimism for the future.

The best part? You become living proof that there's life after covert narcissistic abuse. Not just survival but honest, joyful, authentic living. Your very existence becomes hope for others still finding their way.

And here's the most profound truth about thriving: Setting boundaries and choosing distance isn't just an act of self-love - it's the kindest thing you can do for the covert narcissist, too. This act of setting boundaries empowers you and puts you in control of your own growth and healing journey.

When we continue to engage, enable, and smooth things over, we prevent any possibility of their growth. By walking away, by keeping our distance, by refusing to play the old games, we create space for potential reflection.

Think about it: How many of us had to hit a bottom, face a loss, or experience consequences before we were willing to examine our own behavior? I know in my own life, it was often the people who stepped back, refused to enable me, and gave me the gift of facing myself. It wasn't comfortable, it wasn't easy, but it was necessary for growth.

By staying and trying to fix things, we actually rob covert narcissists of the opportunity to face themselves. Our silence and distance might be the first time they've had to sit with the consequences of their behavior. They might never take that opportunity for self-reflection - but that's not our responsibility.

Being the world's light doesn't mean burning ourselves to keep others warm. Sometimes, it means stepping back and letting natural consequences unfold. Sometimes, the most loving thing we can do is create space for others to face their shadows.

This is real spiritual growth - understanding that we serve others best by being authentic, maintaining healthy boundaries, and doing our inner work. Every day, we commit to our own healing and create ripples of possibility for others' healing, too.

Thriving beyond survival means understanding that your healing isn't just for you—it's a gift to the world. You create space for others to do the same whenever you honor your boundaries, speak your truth, or choose authentic living over people-pleasing.

Your journey of recovery and growth might be the mirror someone else needs to see their own possibility for change. Your willingness to face uncomfortable truths might inspire someone else's self-reflection. Your courage to walk away might be the wake-up call someone needs to begin their own inner work.

Remember: You didn't just survive covert narcissistic abuse - you transformed through it. Your scars became wisdom. Your pain became purpose. Your experience has become a light for others. Not because you're perfect but because you're real. You're willing to keep growing, learning, and sharing what you discover, not because you have all the answers.

This is what true thriving looks like - not just healing yourself but becoming part of the healing of others. Not through sacrifice or self-abandonment but through the quiet power of living authentically and letting that authenticity light the way for others.

Epilogue: Your Future is Yours

If you've made it this far, you've been on quite a journey with me. Whether you're just beginning to recognize covert narcissistic patterns in your life, are in the middle of breaking free, or are well along your path to healing, I want you to know something empowering: You've shown incredible strength, more than you might realize.

Think back to who you were when you first picked up this book. Maybe you were questioning your sanity, wondering if you were the problem, trying to understand why you felt so confused and drained. Perhaps you were looking for confirmation that what you experienced was real.

Now you have a deep understanding. You comprehend the game. You see the patterns. You recognize the manipulation tactics. But more importantly, you know that your sensitivity, empathy, and desire to see the best in others aren't weaknesses to be corrected. They're gifts to be protected.

Progressing doesn't imply that you won't encounter another covert narcissist. They exist and are attracted to bright lights like yours. However, you now possess something you didn't have before: awareness. You know what to watch out for. You trust your instincts. You comprehend that 'no' is a complete sentence.

Most importantly, you've realized that healing isn't just about surviving—it's about transformation. It's about leveraging everything you've learned to craft a life that's authentically yours—a life where you can be gloriously, imperfectly you.

Resources and Support

YOUR JOURNEY TOWARD healing and growth is commendable. To support you further, here are some resources tailored to your needs:

When selecting an online therapist, consider the following factors:

- **Specialization:** Ensure the therapist has experience in treating clients who have endured covert narcissistic abuse.
- **Credentials:** Verify their professional qualifications and licensing.
- **Approach:** Discuss therapeutic methods to find alignment with your personal healing preferences.
- **Compatibility:** A strong therapeutic alliance is crucial; feel comfortable discussing your experiences with them.

Finding a therapist experienced in covert narcissistic abuse is crucial. Here are some professionals online who specialize in this area:

PSYCHOLOGY TODAY'S Therapist Directory – Please Search on a Search Engine to Find These Remarkable Resources:

- Psychology Today keeps a comprehensive directory of therapists specializing in narcissistic personality issues. You can filter your search to find professionals offering online services across various states.

- **Counseling at the Well**

Theresia Richardson, MAEd, LMHC, CCTP is a Licensed Mental Health Counselor specializing in individual, couples and group therapy, and maintains a private practice in Mill Creek, WA.

Counseling at the Well - Counselingatthewell.com

- **DoMental**
- DoMental offers online therapy services tailored for individuals recovering from narcissistic abuse. Their licensed therapists provide personalized treatment plans to address the unique challenges associated with such experiences.
- **Surviving Narcissism**
- Surviving narcissism provides online counseling for individuals dealing with narcissistic relationships. Their platform connects clients with therapists experienced in navigating the complexities of narcissistic abuse.
- **Martha Digby: Narcissistic Abuse Therapist**
- Martha Digby offers online therapy specializing in narcissistic abuse recovery. With over a decade of experience, she utilizes Brainspotting therapy to facilitate healing and empowerment.
- **Jennifer L. Hillier, M.A., LPC**

- Jennifer Hillier provides online counseling services focusing on narcissistic abuse recovery. Her approach aims to help individuals regain their mental health and well-being after experiencing such abuse.

- **Nicole Franco Counseling**

- Nicole Franco offers therapy for individuals experiencing or recovering from narcissistic and emotional abuse. Her services include online sessions to accommodate clients nationwide.

- **Dr. Melody Rhode**

- Vancouver, WA
- A Licensed Clinical Psychologist and Marriage and Family Therapist with expertise in treating personality disorders, including narcissism, and integrating psychology with spiritual wisdom for healing.

- **Frances J. Archer, LMHC, MHP, CMHS**[1]

- Spokane, WA
- Specializes in human relations, healthy dynamics, trauma (including narcissistic abuse), and emotional self-regulation, offering a supportive, non-judgmental environment for personal growth.

- **Christine Kay Cuhaciyan, MA, LMHC, MHP**[2]

---

1. https://www.google.com/maps/search/Frances+J.+Archer%2C+LMHC%2C+MHP%2C+CMHS%2C+Spokane%2C+WA
2. https://www.google.com/maps/search/Christine+Kay+Cuhaciyan%2C+MA%2C+LMHC%2C+MHP%2C+Everett%2C+WA

- Everett, WA
- Focuses on women's issues, including recovery from narcissistic abuse, self-esteem, and codependency, providing guidance through challenging relational dynamics.

Support Groups:

Engaging with support groups can provide community and understanding. Here are some options:

- **Online Communities:**
    - *Covert Narcissism Group on Facebook*: A community for survivors of covert narcissistic abuse. Visit Group[3] www.facebook.com/groups/covertnarcissism/
    - *Victims of Narcissistic Abuse (MyNARA) Support Group*: Offers support for those affected by narcissistic abuse. Visit Group[4] www.facebook.com/groups/1173575726175953/
- **Meetup Groups:**
    - *Narcissism Survivor Groups*: Connect with local survivors through Meetup. Explore Groups[5] Narcissism Survivor groups | Meetup[6]

When choosing a support group, look for environments that promote healing and personal growth.

- **Self-Care Resources:**
- Healing encompasses multiple facets. Here are some

3. https://www.facebook.com/groups/covertnarcissism/

4. https://www.facebook.com/groups/1173575726175953/

5. https://www.meetup.com/topics/narcissism-survivor/

6. https://www.meetup.com/topics/narcissism-survivor/

modalities to consider:

- **Somatic Therapy:**
    - *Mindbodyology*: Offers services focused on narcissistic abuse recovery through somatic approaches
- **Meditation and Mindfulness:**
    - *Insight Timer*: A free app with a vast library of guided meditations.
- **Movement Therapies:**
    - *Yoga with Adriene*: Free yoga sessions suitable for all levels.
- **Creative Expression:**
    - *The Artist's Way by Julia Cameron*: A book offering a 12-week program to unlock creativity.
- **Energy Work:**
    - *Healing Touch Program*: Provides information on energy healing modalities.

FINAL THOUGHTS:

Your resilience and commitment to healing are inspiring. Remember, seeking support is a sign of strength. Trust your journey and know that a community is ready to support you. Your future is a canvas; with each authentic choice, you paint a path toward a hopeful future.

You Are Enough

Your journey through understanding and healing from covert narcissistic abuse has taken us through many landscapes - from recognizing the subtle signs and breaking free of trauma bonds to rebuilding your life and finding genuine joy again. We've explored how these relationships form, why empaths are particularly vulnerable, and how to protect your beautiful, giving nature without losing it.

We've learned that healing isn't just about getting over what happened - it's about growing into who you were always meant to be. It's about reclaiming your voice, trusting your intuition, and creating boundaries that protect your spirit while keeping your heart open.

Through every chapter, we've seen how covert narcissistic abuse differs from more apparent forms of manipulation, how it can appear in any relationship - personal, professional, or familial - and how it slowly erodes our sense of self while making us question our own reality.

But most importantly, we've discovered that surviving this experience doesn't have to make us harder—it can make us wiser. Our sensitivity, when properly protected, is still our greatest gift. Our ability to care, when matched with healthy boundaries, is still our superpower.

And here's the truth that brings it all together: You didn't just survive a covert narcissist - you graduated from one of life's most profound teachers. Your wounds have become wisdom. Your pain has become purpose. Your experience has become a light for others. In choosing to heal, in doing this deep work, in reclaiming your authentic self, you haven't just changed your own life - you've become part of the healing of the world. Every time one chooses to break these patterns, live authentically, and thrive beyond survival, they create a ripple of possibility that touches countless others. This is how we heal the world - one authentic, courageous heart at a time.

About the Author

Nicole Elizabeth Orozco earned her undergraduate degree in Psychology from Chapman University, where her fascination with Jungian psychology and the collective unconscious first took root. While life's path led her away from pursuing a PsyD at Pacifica Graduate Institute, it guided her toward a rich journey of personal development and transformational studies that would ultimately shape her writing and professional path.

As the founder and CEO of Elixir Publishing House, Nicole combines her extensive background in personal development with professional publishing services. She offers transformational coaching, ghostwriting, and publishing guidance to aspiring authors. Her upcoming course offerings will further expand her mission of helping others share their stories and wisdom with the world.

Drawing from her extensive career as a counselor, teacher, and program director for the mentally ill, Nicole has spent decades helping others navigate their inner worlds and achieve personal growth. Her first book, The Single Mother's Journey to Wholeness (2005), received the Editor's Choice award and established her voice in transformational literature. Later, as a newspaper publisher, she developed a passion for sharing stories that inspire reflection and deeper understanding. Nicole's diverse career background is a testament to her expertise and experience, reassuring readers of her ability to guide them on their personal transformation journeys.

Nicole's work is influenced by her studies in psychology and philosophical traditions, including the teachings of Carl Jung and Joseph Campbell. She weaves together academic insight with practical wisdom to create narratives and coaching programs that facilitate meaningful personal transformation and offer tools for self-discovery and healing.

Nicole firmly believes that personal transformation is the key to creating positive change in the world and securing a brighter future for our children and grandchildren. Through Elixir Publishing House (elixirpublishinghouse.com), she is dedicated to guiding others on their transformational journeys, offering a unique blend of psychology and practical personal development that makes complex concepts accessible to people from all walks of life. Her work is a testament to the power of personal transformation, empowering individuals to take charge of their lives and make a difference.

Residing in a suburb of Seattle, Washington, Nicole is dedicated to expanding her influence as an author, publisher, and transformational coach. As a wife, mother, and grandmother, she is unwavering in her mission to foster a world where individual growth leads to collective healing, ensuring a brighter future for the next generations. Her current project, the next book in The Soul Factory series, is a testament to her enduring commitment.

www.ingramcontent.com/pod-product-compliance
Lightning Source LLC
LaVergne TN
LVHW090414210926
848480LV00002B/559